Madame Jeanne Guyon:
Her Autobiography

Madame Jeanne Guyon: Her Autobiography

Edited by Jan Johnson

SeedSowers Publishing
Jacksonville, Florida

Madame Jeanne Guyon:
Her Autobiography Condensed and Modernized
Copyright © 1998
Jan Johnson

Published by SeedSowers
Christian Books Publishing House
4003 N Liberty Street
Jacksonville, FL 32206
www.seedsowers.com
800-228-2665

Printed in the United States of America

ISBN: 978-0-9797515-2-3
       0-9797515-2-7

Books by Jeanne Guyon

Experiencing the Depths of Jesus Christ
Union With God
Final Steps in Christian Maturity
Intimacy With Christ
Spiritual Torrents
The Autobiography of Jeanne Guyon

Commentaries by Jeanne Guyon

Exodus
Genesis
Leviticus–Numbers–Deuteronomy
Judges
Job
Song of Songs
Jeremiah
James–I John–Revelation

Biography of Jeanne Guyon

The Life of Jeanne Guyon (Upham)

A Little Bird I Am

A little bird I am,
Shut from the fields of air;
And in my cage I sit and sing
To Him who placed me there;
Well pleased a prisoner to be,
Because, my God, it pleases Thee.

Nought have I else to do;
I sing the whole day long;
And He whom most I love to please,
Doth listen to my song;
He caught and bound my wandering wing,
But He still bends to hear me sing.

Thou hast an ear to hear;
A heart to love and bless;
And, though my notes were e'er so rude,
Thou wouldst not hear the less;
Because Thou knowest, as they fall,
That Love, sweet Love, inspires them all.

My cage confines me round;
Abroad I cannot fly;
But though my wing is closely bound,
My heart's at liberty.
My prison walls cannot control
The flight, the freedom of the soul.

Table of Contents

Introduction

Have you ever read a book that impressed you, and you wondered, *How did this author acquire such a deep knowledge of God? What did this person do or what happened to this person to make them experience life within God this way?* That's how I felt when I first read *Experiencing the Depths of Jesus Christ* by Jeanne Guyon. Fortunately for us, she wrote an autobiography that informs us of how she knew what she knew.

This is a tale of a beautiful, witty, wealthy woman, Jeanne-Marie Bouvier de la Mothe Guyon. Although doted on by her religious, highly-esteemed father, she suffered much rejection in childhood, changing the place she called home nine times in ten years. An early marriage offered more rejection, and she became a widow at twenty-eight.

For the rest of her life, she suffered persecution and endured imprisonments primarily because she believed all Christians could have a rich, interior life of prayer. She wrestled to find a relationship with God and then commend it to others in an era when the church valued reasoning of the mind and internal politics much more. When a religious organization demanded her money and vast estate, she gave them up.

She gave generously to the poor and oppressed and spent time guiding souls to God, yet neither of these things spared her persecution.

Jeanne Guyon wrote this work from a lonely prison cell just as John Bunyan and the apostle Paul did. She did not write to broadcast her sufferings and triumphs, but because she was ordered to do so. In fact, she was told to "omit nothing from the account," and the rules of the church forced her to obey this command. Under this pressure, she described her "crosses" and ecstasies with an objectivity that astonishes us. We expect her to downplay both her suffering and the astounding miracles God did through her, but she related them candidly in submission to an authority she respected even though it persecuted her.

Cultural Jump for Us

As you read this book, expect to enter a different world. Louis XIV was king of seventeenth century France and enjoyed a depraved court life that nevertheless claimed to be intensely religious. All of Europe was recovering from the Thirty Years' War, which brought disillusionment with religious institutions. Alongside this, the Renaissance was giving way to scientific rationalism. These two forces—dissatisfaction with religion and fascination with intellect—pressured the church to remain respectable in the face of scientific thought. The result was that reasoning of the mind crowded out any religion of the heart. People like Jeanne Guyon who sought to experience God in prayer were viewed as antiques or even a threat to the future of the church. If the church destabilized, this could bring down the government. If the government fell, the ambitious members of nobility would lose their wealth. This brought her many enemies.

But Jeanne Guyon's inward spirituality was not the only issue that led to her persecution. She was wealthy and in her widowhood was willing to detach herself from her wealth, and so greedy royalty, nobility and churchmen alike saw this as an opportunity to acquire her wealth for themselves. She allowed this and could have been free, but she would not allow them to compromise the inheritance of her daughter.

You may find yourself thinking, *Stand up for yourself, woman!* but a woman in that era had little power. Jeanne Guyon lived in subservience to ecclesiastical leaders and was fiercely loyal to her church, its leaders, and her country, France. She subjected herself to a "spiritual director," often taking his words as the voice of God. (Spiritual directors are persons trained to help others follow God in their life. They carried great authority in those days.) She did, in fact, speak up against church authorities who thought public prayers could be made only by professionals of the church. She counseled paupers and high church officials alike.

Another cultural leap requires understanding that she lived in an age of a rigid class system. Although you and I might question whether this woman of nobility needed servants and nannies—even in prison—this was her legal right at that time. Compared to others of her class in that day, she was caring and open-hearted to her servants. Never a physically strong person, Jeanne Guyon was often sick and managed quite well for someone in her condition.

You may also think, *Get out of town, woman! Save yourself!* but that culture was not as mobile as ours. If people, especially women, found themselves in impossible situations, they could not just pick up and leave. Transportation was difficult and strangers were targets for treachery.

How This Story Can Help

When I began working on this story, I thought this woman I had admired for so long, Jeanne Guyon, was strange. But as I progressed, I found that what makes her so different is that she truly believed and acted upon the truth that *all things work together for good for those who love God.* She believed much more than I that God is in charge of bizarre situations—an impossible marriage, a perilous journey, a greedy relative, a harsh bureaucracy. It wasn't that she didn't stand up for herself, but that she didn't choose to interfere with what she believed to be God's hand at work. So as I edited her words, I saw myself change. It was easier to accept what I didn't like in life. I was more willing to wait and watch for God. I experimented more with letting go. I even thanked God for a terrible headache one day which dulled my thinking so much that I didn't return the anger of a loved one.

So I recommend this story to you especially if you're in the middle of enduring an impossible situation. God may use it to help you see His hand at work even in the smallest things, even turning other's evil for your good.

This book, then, adds to the great literature of similar authors such as John of the Cross and Brother Lawrence. It's interesting that the latter's book, *The Practice of the Presence of God,*[1] was published a few years after Jeanne Guyon's book,

---

[1] Modernized and published by Seedsowers under the title *Practicing His Presence.*

Experiencing the Depths of Jesus Christ, and a few years before she was imprisoned the second time. Both of these authors emphasized constant communication with God and the necessary abandonment of self. Those themes met a need in their times as well as our own.

1

A "Lively" Child

I am doing as I have been asked—writing this autobiography—although the labor is painful since I cannot study or reflect easily these days. I do wish, however, to paint in true colors the goodness of God to me. I wrote an earlier history of myself in which I mostly described my faults and said little of God's favors. I was ordered to burn it and to write another. In this one, I am to omit nothing that has befallen me—even the remarkable things, scarcely to be believed. I've been asked not to list my sins, so I shall instead declare the favors of the Lord our God and magnify His mercies.

This story shows how devotion to God comes from pain and weariness. When God builds His sacred temple within us, He first totally razes our pompous self, and from its ruins He forms a new structure.

God's mystery and the secrets of God's conduct are hidden from the wise of the world, who view themselves as God's helpers. They claim through wisdom and intelligence to comprehend the height and depth and length and breadth of God, but they are enveloped in their own works. Wisdom that emanates from God is found only in dying to all things and being truly lost to them so we can move toward God and exist only in Him.

I was born Jeanne-Marie Bouvier de la Mothe on April 18, 1648, in the town of Montargis.[2] When my mother was eight months' pregnant with me, something frightened her and she went into premature labor. Children born so early don't usually survive, and so they thought I would die. When it looked as if I would live, they sent for a priest to baptize me, only to stop because I again appeared to be dying. Because of these early troubles, my health has always been fragile.

A Child in the Convent

I continued to be quite sickly until I was two and a half years old, when they sent me to live in a convent for a few months. On my return, my mother paid little attention to my education. She was not fond of daughters and left me to be cared for by servants. God, however, was my protector because even though I was sickly, I was also lively. I frequently got into accidents such as falling into a deep pit that held our firewood, but I always escaped unhurt.

When I was about four years old, a friend of my father, Monsieur De la Mothe, who was a religious man, urged him to send me to a convent to live with my half sister. She delighted in my sweetness and mischievousness, and I became her constant companion. I was always getting into scrapes, but I conducted myself well when I had no one to lead me astray. I loved to hear

---

[2] This date does not agree with her later statement that August 22, 1688 was her birthday (p. 128 of this book). Nor does it agree with Thomas C. Upham *Life of Madame Guyon* (London: Allenson & Co., LTD, 1905), p. 1.

about God and to be at church, and especially to be dressed in religious garb.

On one occasion, to tone down my liveliness, a caregiver told me about the terrors of hell. The next night I dreamed of hell, and I have never forgotten it. I saw horrible darkness where souls were punished as they pointed to my place among them. I wept bitterly and cried to God that I would behave better.

O Lord, Thou did hearken to my cry and poured strength and courage on me to serve even as a child.

After this dream, I wanted to go to confession privately, but because I was so young, the mistress of the girls carried me to the priest and stayed while I was heard. She was astonished when she heard me say I had doubts, but the priest laughed and asked me what they were. I told him how I'd doubted there was a hell and how I'd thought my mistress made it up to get me to behave. But since my dream, I believed!

Failed Martyrdom

After confession, my heart glowed and I decided I wanted to be a martyr for God. The girls who lived at the convent amused themselves by trying to see how far my fervor for God would carry me. They offered to prepare me for martyrdom, and I was so pleased with my new religious passion that I begged them to kill me so I could enter into God's sacred presence.

So I knelt on a cloth spread out for my death (the cloth would absorb the blood), and as I saw a large sword being lifted up behind me, I cried, "Stop! It's wrong to die without getting my father's permission first." The girls then scolded me for saying this just so I could escape the sword. Since I'd gotten out of being a martyr, I felt sad. Something reproved me inwardly for not choosing heaven when I could have had it so easily.

Because I was sick so frequently, I asked to be taken home. But while there, I went whole days without seeing my mother while she paid attention to my brother. I felt so hurt that I stayed away from her. It is true my brother was more amiable than I, but she was so excessively fond of him that she was blind to my good qualities. She saw only my faults.

My father loved me tenderly and wanted me to be educated, so he sent me back to the convent when I was almost seven years old. My two half sisters lived there—one by my father, the other by my mother. My father placed me under the care of his daughter because she was devoted to God and a fit teacher. This was a special show of God's providence because my sister loved me tenderly, which helped her see my amiable qualities.

This good sister instructed me well, giving up her personal time to be with me. If I answered her questions correctly (more from chance than understanding), she felt rewarded for her labor. Under her care, I mastered my studies.

My father often sent for me to come home, and on one visit, when I was nearly eight, the Queen of England was there. My father invited the queen's priest to amuse himself by asking me difficult questions. When he did, I gave such fitting answers that he took me to the queen and said, "Your Majesty will enjoy this child." She was so pleased with me that she demanded that my father give me to her to be groomed as a woman of the royal court. My father resisted. Doubtless God influenced this refusal, for how could I have withstood the temptations and distractions of a court life?

I went back to my good sister at the convent, but I often went along with the other girls boarding there and picked up bad habits—lying, moodiness, indifference, passing whole days without thinking on God. My sister's care quickly influenced me again, and I loved to hear of God and pray. I liked going to church and developed tenderness for the poor.

At the end of the convent's garden, there was a chapel. I went there to pray and sometimes took my breakfast to sacrifice it to Christ, hiding it behind the statue of Christ. I did this to humble myself, but my self-love often kept me from doing it. When they were cleaning out the chapel, they found all I had left behind the statue and guessed I had done it. I believe God was pleased with my infantile devotion.

Troubles with my Sisters and Brother

Life was easy with that sister. She taught me whenever I was well, but I often was seized with sudden, uncommon illnesses. In the evening I would feel fine, but in the morning I became feverish and swelled up and developed bluish marks. At nine years, I was taken with such violent bleeding that they thought I would die.

In the meantime, my other sister (on the maternal side) became jealous, wanting her turn to care for me. She wasn't as skilled an instructor as my paternal sister, so I didn't respond as well to her. She also saw that I loved my paternal sister better, so she didn't allow me to speak to my other sister. When she knew I had spoken to her, she had me whipped, or she beat me herself. I could not hold out against her, and so I no longer went to see my paternal sister. But she continued to be good to me, especially when I was sick. She understood my fear of being punished for seeing her.

When my father was informed of this, he took me home. I was nearly ten years old by then, but after a little while, another friend of my father's, a prioress (leader of nuns), urged him to place me in her convent, which he did.

While there, I caught the chicken pox and stayed in bed for three weeks, but the women of the house feared it was smallpox, so they did not come near me. I saw almost no one, so I found a Bible and read it from morning to night, especially the historical parts. But I was never happy at this house. The older girls picked on me, and I got so little food that I became emaciated.

After about eight months my father took me home. My mother gave me more attention, but she still preferred my brother. If I was sick and wanted a certain thing, he would demand it, and it would be taken from me and given to him. He beat me and one time threw me down from the top of the coach, but his behavior was winked at. This soured my temper, and I stopped wanting to be good.

I looked with jealousy on my brother. Whatever he did was appreciated, but if blame was in the air, it fell on me. My stepsister by my mother gained her favor by catering to him and persecuting me. True, I was bad. I relapsed into lying and moodiness. I prayed to God, loved to hear any one speak of Him, and loved being charitable to the poor. Yet sin grew more powerful in me. I closed up the avenues of my heart so I could not hear that secret voice of God calling me to Himself.

O my God, Thy grace seemed to double with my sin! It was as if Thou attacked a walled city. Thou did surround my heart, but I raised defenses, adding every day to my wrongs to prevent Thee taking it. When Thou appeared to win over my ungrateful heart, I raised a counter-attack, and threw up barricades to keep off Thy goodness and to stop your flow of grace. No one could have conquered me, but Thee.

Not only did my brother trouble me, but the girl assigned to care for me beat me when fixing my hair. My father would have stopped this if he had known, but I told him nothing because I feared him as well as loved him. I loved reading and shut myself up alone every day to read without interruption. When my mother complained of me, he always replied, "There are twelve hours in the day; she'll grow wiser."

Mademoiselle de la Mothe

As I grew tall for my age, my mother became more pleased with me. She dressed me well and brought good company to our home and took me with her traveling abroad. She took pride in the beauty God gave me. I perverted that beauty into a source of pride. Several suitors came to me, but my father did not listen to any proposals since I was not yet twelve years old.

When my father saw how tall I had grown, he placed me in the convent to receive my first Communion at Easter. My most dear sister prepared me for this act of devotion. I thought now of giving myself to God in earnest—to be a nun. I often felt a war going on between my good intentions and bad habits. So I did penances.

When Easter arrived, I received Communion with joy and devotion. Then my other sister demanded I join her class. Her manners, so opposite of my paternal sister's ways, caused me to step back from my former devotion to God. I no longer felt that new and delightful ardor which had seized my heart at my first Communion. Alas! My faults and failings soon repeated themselves and drew me away from religion.

What helped me at this time was the visit of my father's nephew. He came to see us on his way to a mission to Cochin China (now Vietnam). I was taking a walk with my companions while he was there. When I returned, he was gone. I was so touched by his devotion (as they described it to me) that I cried the rest of the day. Early in the morning I went in great distress to seek the priest. I said to him, "I don't want to be the only person in our family to be lost. Help me in my salvation."

After that, I became so changed others scarcely knew me. I tried to make no mistakes, and when I discovered the smallest faults, God helped me conquer them. As soon as I upset anyone, including the servants, I begged their pardon, which subdued my wrath and pride.

I gave all I had to the poor, taking expensive linen to their houses. I taught them the catechism, and when my parents dined out, I asked the poor to eat with me and served them with great respect.

I read great religious works, and in them I learned what inward prayer was. I asked my priest to teach me that kind of prayer, but he did not, so I worked out my own methods. I was not good at it. So I concluded it was too difficult, which troubled me for a long time. I earnestly asked God to give me the gift of prayer, as I would do many times more.

2

My Decisions Made for Me

Now I knew I wanted to become a nun. Often I stole out of my father's house and begged the nuns of a nearby community to receive me into their convent. Though they wanted to let me join them, they did not because they feared my father, whose fondness for me was well known.

At that convent lived a niece of my father, and I owe this cousin a great deal. She told my father how I desired to join the convent, and he cried. (Families in those days often gave their first born to the church, but her parents had already done that with her older half sisters.) When he happened to be abroad, I pleaded with my mother, but she would not consent for fear of grieving my father.

Into the Convent?

My cousin supported me with love and kindness, which made my mother jealous. She feared I would love my cousin too much and her too little. So my mother, who had stayed away from me in my young years and left me with servants, now wanted me to be with her at all times. When my cousin fell ill, my mother sent her home, which was a severe blow to my heart as well as to the movement of God in me.

My mother, however, was truly a virtuous and charitable woman. She gave away not only the surplus in our house, but the necessities. She gave poor mechanics tools to carry on their work and needy tradesmen what they needed in their shops. She sometimes gave the last penny in the house even though she had a large family to maintain.

About this time I noticed God gave me grace to forgive grievances—it surprised my priest! Some young ladies had slandered me, but I spoke well of them. I continued in this frame of mind of perseverance as long as I practiced inward prayer.

A Distraction from Inward Prayer

When we went to the country on vacation, my father took with us a young gentleman who was accomplished in many ways. He wanted to marry me, but my father put him off since he was such a close relative. He offered prayers every day, and because I liked saying prayers with him, I quit practicing inward prayer.

I did not see this was the Enemy's strategy to draw me away from God and entangle me in more snares. My spirit gradually decayed, not being nourished by prayer, and I became cold toward God. All my old faults revived, to which I added an excessive vanity. The love I had for myself choked the little love I had left for God.

Oh, my God, if people understood the great value to the soul from conversing with Thee, everyone would be diligent in it. Children are told to attain heaven and avoid hell, yet they are not taught the shortest and easiest way of arriving at it—inward prayer.

When I stopped practicing inward prayer, I abandoned a fountain of living water. I became like a vineyard exposed to thieves with hedges torn down so that anyone could ravage it. I began to seek in human friendship what I had found in God. God left me to myself because I first left him. By letting me sink into the horrible pit, I felt the importance of seeking God in prayer.

Conceit and corruption took over my heart. I constantly stood before the mirror and enjoyed viewing myself so much that I thought others should do the same. I looked beautiful to myself because I could not see my polluted soul within. I became more self-willed than before, and I frequently lied.

My high opinion of myself made me find fault in others. In myself I saw only my good qualities, and in others only defects. I hid my faults from myself, and the few I found seemed small in comparison to others' faults. I even rationalized them to myself as positives. I read romances excessively, spending whole days and nights at them. Sometimes dawn came while I continued to read so that for a while I stopped sleeping. I wanted to get to the end of the book to satisfy a craving within me.

Meanwhile, God knocked at the door of my heart. I shed tears over how different I was from when I enjoyed God's sacred presence. But my tears were fruitless because I could not get out of this wretched state by myself. I wished some loving, powerful hand would pull me out. When I tried to pull myself out, I sunk deeper, and each fruitless attempt made me see my own powerlessness and left me more troubled.

As I became of marriageable age, my father moved our family to Paris. My parents spared no cost in presenting me as an advantageous bride. So my vanity increased, and I paraded my beauty whenever I could. I wanted to be loved by everyone but loved no one but myself. Several good offers of marriage were made for me, but God did not permit these matters to succeed.

M. Jacques Guyon, a man of great wealth,[3] had asked for me in marriage for several years, but my father always refused him. Yet my father grew afraid I would run off with Monsieur Guyon because of his riches, so he and my mother reluctantly promised me to him. But they didn't tell me. I signed the marriage articles without knowing what they were.

I did not see my future husband until a few days before our marriage. Everyone in the village rejoiced at my wedding but me. I was so depressed I did not laugh or eat. And I did not know why. Then my desire to be a nun came pouring in. All who came to wish me well the next day tried to cheer me up, but I wept bitterly. I answered, "I wanted to be a nun. Why am I married? How could such a fate befall me?"

A Child in Her Own Household

At the time of my marriage, I was just fifteen years old and my husband was thirty-seven. As soon as I went to live in his home, I sensed it would be a house of mourning for me. His family lived so differently from mine. At the home of my father, we had lived with great elegance, but Monsieur Guyon's mother had been a widow for a long time and regarded thriftiness as

---

3 Upham, p. 18.

most important. My family spoke in a genteel, courteous way, but when I spoke this way, my husband's family said I was trying to teach them how to talk. If questions were posed at my father's house, he encouraged me to speak freely. In my new home, if I spoke up, they said I was starting a dispute!

It seemed as though I was scolded from morning till night. My mother-in-law opposed me and made me perform humiliating tasks. She saw all my faults but admitted none of her own. She worked at thwarting me and inspired these feelings in her son. They gave persons who were my inferiors a place above me. This hurt my mother, who had a high sense of honor. When she heard it from others (for I told her nothing), she chided me, thinking I did not know how to keep my rank and had no spirit. I dared not tell her how I was ready to die from grief and frustration.

Dislike for My Family

My husband and mother-in-law also spoke against my father and my relatives. I took this harder than what they said about me. I defended my parents, but this provoked my husband and his mother even more. Anyone who complained about my family was instantly liked. Anyone who showed friendship to me was not welcome in my new home. A relative I loved came to see me, and they made her leave.

It became difficult to visit my parents because when I returned I heard bitter speeches about it. My mother then complained that I did not come to see her often enough. She said I did not love her, that I was alienated from my family and too attached to my husband.

What increased my anguish was that my mother told my mother-in-law how I had given her pains from infancy. Together they decided I had an evil spirit, so my husband would not let me be by myself. He forced me to stay all day with my mother-in-law. She criticized me to others, lessening their affection for me. However, most people saw me bear it patiently and developed a high regard for me.

In the rare times I was allowed to be by myself, I cried. When they were in a rage, I begged their pardon even though I could not figure out what I did wrong.

By her constant criticism, my mother-in-law found the secret of extinguishing my liveliness and making me look stupid. Some of my former acquaintances hardly knew me anymore. Those who had not met me before said, "Is this the person famed for her wit? She can't say two words." I was not yet sixteen years old, but I was so intimidated that I didn't go anywhere without my mother-in-law yet was too fearful to speak in her presence.

In this marriage, I was more a slave than a free person. My husband was plagued with gout twice in the first year of our marriage, six weeks each time. He did not come out of his room or get out of bed. I took care of him, but he did not become warm toward me. I gave up small pleasures to be with my husband. My friends told me I was too young to be nursing someone who was becoming an invalid.

When I left the house, the footmen on the coach had orders to report back everything I did. At the dinner table, something always happened to bring me to tears. For the most part, I patiently bore these things, but sometimes I let a hasty answer escape me. I had no one to confide in, and I resolved to tell no one.

Sometimes my husband quietly put up with me, and I felt happy. At other times I seemed unbearable to him. Yet when anyone (besides my mother-in-law) said anything against me, he flew into a rage, for he loved me so much. When I was sick, he was inconsolable. I believe that without my mother-in-law's influence we would have been very happy together.

(I fear I'm not being kind by saying all this, but I have been asked not to omit any detail, so I do not. Even though my husband's family treated me this way, they were good people. My husband's mother was virtuous and had good sense. My husband had religion and no vices. He loved me passionately, but he was rash and hasty, and my mother-in-law continually taunted him about me.

Besides, it is important to view this through God's eyes. He permitted these things to help me. I was so filled with pride that if they had treated me better, my pride would have multiplied and perhaps I would never have turned to God as these multitude of crosses forced me to do.)

> *These things Thou hast arranged, O my God, to help*
> *me to die to my pride. I could not have destroyed it myself,*
> *but Thou accomplished it by Thy providence.*

The Turbulent Maid

To complete my distress, I was given a maid who watched me like a governess. She often demeaned me, and when I asked her pardon, she triumphed, saying, "I knew I was right."

Sometimes she ran out into the street, crying out against me. One time she exclaimed, "I am so unhappy to have such a terrible mistress!" People gathered about her and asked what I'd done, and not knowing what to say, she answered that I had not spoken to her all the day. They laughed and said, "She's done you no harm."

One day, as she waited on me, she yelled at me and jerked my clothing. I said, "You are causing me no pain, but because you're mistreating me, your mistress, God is undoubtedly offended by you." She ran like a mad woman, telling my husband she was leaving. She said I was jealous of her because she took care of him when he was sick.

My husband became angry at these words and came at me like a lion, threatening me with his uplifted crutch. I thought he was going to knock me down, so I waited for the blow with tranquility, united to God. He didn't strike me but threw the crutch at me. He then yelled at me as if I were a street beggar. I kept silent and gathered myself to God.

In the meantime, the maid came in. At the sight of her, his rage doubled. I crouched near to God, ready to suffer whatever He permitted. My husband ordered me to beg her pardon, which I did, and that appeased him. I think he did this out of loyalty to her for the way she took care of him.

About six months after I was married, I was so grieved that I was tempted to cut out my tongue so that I might not irritate them any more. When I could be alone I cried, and my grief became more bitter every day. These blows took the liveliness out of my nature so that I became like a lamb that is shorn. I prayed to our Lord to help me, and He was my refuge. As I was so much younger than they (twenty-two years younger than my husband), I knew their dispositions would not change.

Returning to God

Such heavy crosses made me return to God. I still had pride, but my troubles made me try to correct my life. I stopped reading romances and began reading the Gospels. I resumed the practice of prayer and felt His love emerge in my heart.

Yet during the first year of our marriage, I continued to struggle with vanity. I sometimes lied to get away from my husband and mother-in-law. I see now how their unreasonable conduct was necessary for me. Had I been praised as I was at my father's house, I would have grown intolerably proud. Their criticism curbed my old fault of criticizing other woman who were praised.

> *In this deplorable condition, O my God, I saw I needed Thy help. For at that tender age, I could have been drawn away by these domestic crosses. But Thou, by Thy goodness and love, did draw me to Thyself. Thou made use of my natural pride, forcing me to live so honorably that my husband knew my innocence and didn't believe my mother-in-law's accusations.*

3

"Seek God in Your Heart and You Will Find Him"

I welcomed childbirth because I became gravely ill, and so my husband and mother-in-law were nice to me. They took care of me because they wanted an heir to inherit their fortunes. My crosses were lessened a bit, but as my time of delivery drew near, this tenderness lessened. Once, I pretended to have colic just to alarm them, but I saw that my play-acting gave them too much pain, so I told them I was better.

I gave birth to a son, Armand Jacques Guyon.[4] After my delivery, I remained weak and took a fever. Then a painful abscess fell upon my breast, which was laid open in two places. I could not bear to be moved. These sicknesses were but a shadow of the pain I felt in life with this family.

Yet the sickness also improved my appearance, which increased my conceit. I loved hearing compliments. When I walked in the streets of Paris, reveling in its sights and sounds, I pulled off my hat out of vanity. I pulled off my gloves to show

---

[4] Upham, p. 27.

my hands. Could there be greater folly? After falling into these weaknesses, I used to weep bitterly at home. Yet I fell into them again.

Family Financial Troubles

My husband then lost some money, which made life difficult because my mother-in-law blamed me. She said that no afflictions fell on them until I came into the house. In my mind I excused my mother-in-law, thinking that if I'd been the one to scrape and save for years, I would be upset too.

We met with loss after loss, the king reducing our income and demanding great sums of money from us (to meet his military and court life expenses[5]). I had no peace in these afflictions and no confidante. My mother died about this time, and my dear half sister had died two months before my marriage.

During one of my husband's long absences on business, I felt so vexed that I wanted to go after him, but my mother-in-law opposed it. This time my father insisted, so she let me go. When I arrived, I found he had almost died from lack of care. Riddled with worry, he couldn't finish his work, so he hid himself at a hotel. He didn't want my presence to reveal his whereabouts, so he told me to go home. Finally he let me stay in hiding with him because he had missed me for so long.

Outwardly everything appeared agreeable, but my husband was so overcome with setbacks that he was continually upset. Sometimes he threatened to throw our supper out the window,

---

5 Upham, p. 27.

so I teased him that it would be unfair since I had such a keen appetite! Then he laughed. God gave me patience and grace with his hasty words. The devil, who attempted to make me feel offended, was forced to go away confused in the face of my patience.

Again, I dislike saying so many things against my mother-in-law. I have no doubt my lack of discretion, my notions, and my occasionally rash temper drew many of the crosses upon me. I see now that at that time my crosses did not yet come from Christ, but from my own vain behavior.

In this distress, I prayed twice a day and continually asked God to tame my spirit. I went to visit the poor in their houses, assisting them in their distresses. I did all the good I knew to do. I began dressing and fixing my hair modestly, and I rarely looked in the mirror. I confined my reading to books of devotion. I let my turbulent maid dress me however she pleased, which lessened the friction between us. This also took away reasons for me to feel vain. The more indifferent I was about dress, the better I was in my heart. I often examined myself very strictly, writing down my faults from week to week to see how much I was improved or reformed. Alas! These lists didn't help because I trusted in my own efforts.

Visitors to My Father's House

A lady who had been exiled came to my father for help, and he offered her an apartment there. She had great inward devotion and saw that I desired to love God. She complimented the goodness of my outward life but said I had not yet attained simplicity in prayer. The way she acted and the expressions on her face showed me how much she enjoyed God's presence. I tried to achieve this too, but could not. Later I realized I tried to acquire by my own efforts what I could have only by ceasing from all effort.

This exiled lady stayed for quite a while and was there when my father's nephew returned from Cochin China (Vietnam). They talked about the art of praying continually, but I couldn't understand how they managed to do this. I tried to meditate and think on God continually, but I could not. He complimented me, saying that I had an unusual devotion to God for one of my accomplishments and position in society. While others my age (I was not yet eighteen) were relishing pleasures of society, I was interested in prayer. Yet I complained to my father's nephew of my faults, but he advised me to be more positive and to persevere. He would have introduced me to a more simple manner of prayer, but I was not ready for it.

The desire I had to please Thee—the tears I shed and the pains I took with no fruit—moved Thee with compassion. Beholding how I toiled, Thou turned in my favor, and Thy breath carried me full sail over this sea of affliction.

Shortly after that visit, God permitted a man of the Franciscan religious order to visit my father's house. He had intended to go a shorter way but changed his plans. He thought God had called him to convert a man of distinction near my father's house, but this labor proved fruitless. I believe the conquest of my soul was God's plan!

When the Franciscan arrived, I was about to give birth to my second son, so I didn't think it was proper to visit him, but my father urged me to see him anyway. To show respect, I took a female relative with me as a chaperone. At first he seemed confused, for he was reserved toward women. Having just come out of five years of solitude, he was surprised that a young woman was the first person to call on him for help. He said nothing for a while and then, "Madame, you seek without what you have within. Accustom yourself to seek God in your heart, and there you will find Him."

Then the Franciscan left the room. These words pierced my heart like a dart and showed me what I had been seeking for so many years. I had made my lists and sought God in outward activities, but I had not simply enjoyed God in my heart.

O my Lord, Thou was in my heart, and demanded only a simple turning of my mind inward, to make me sense Thy presence. How I was running hither and thither to seek Thee. My life was a burden. I sought Thee where Thou was not, and did not seek Thee where thou was indeed. I did not understand the words of Thy Gospel, "The kingdom of God is within you."

I went to find this devout Franciscan man and told him my heart was changed, that I experienced God's presence in my soul. I felt my soul anointed and healed in a moment of all wounds. I did not sleep that night because God's love flowed in me like oil. It burned in me as a fire devouring all that was left of self. As time passed, I seemed different to myself and others. My troublesome faults disappeared, being consumed like debris in a great fire.

Finally, I decided I wanted to ask the Franciscan to be my spiritual director. He excused himself, saying that I was too young (nineteen years old) and that he had promised God (out of distrust of himself) never to direct a woman unless God charged him to do so. However, he agreed to pray and asked that I pray. As he prayed, he heard from God: "Fear not this person; she is My spouse." When he told me this, I thought, *How can God call me His spouse? I am a frightful monster of iniquity who has offended God!* After this, the Franciscan consented to be my spiritual director.

Ecstasy of Inward Prayer

At this time, nothing was easier for me than prayer. Hours passed like moments, and I loved God without interrupting thoughts. This rejoicing prayer didn't involve a lot of concentration. The taste of God was so pure and constant that it drew my soul into a profound reflection. I saw nothing but Jesus Christ alone, and selfish motives faded.

When we went to the country on business, I was so insatiable for prayer that I arose at four o'clock in the morning to pray. The church was situated such that the coach could not get to it, so I walked down a steep hill to get there and back up to come back. But I didn't mind because I had such a longing desire to meet with God. If I went among people, I often could not speak because I was preoccupied within. I took some needle work to hide behind so my heart could stay focused.

I loved God without thinking about what gifts or favors God might give me in return. The Beloved Himself attracted my heart. Pleasures that others loved much appeared dull to me. I wondered how I could ever have enjoyed them.

I noticed how this prayer of the heart gave me stronger faith. I was fearful and intimidated before, but now feared nothing. I felt confidence in God, wanting to do His will and respect the sovereignty of God over me. I understood these words: "My yoke is easy, and my burden is light" (Matt. 11:30).

From that time forward, I desired to be wholly devoted to God—whatever that meant. I said to God, "Thou could not command anything of me I would not give." I viewed my crosses as occasions for putting my devotion to the test.

Unusual Effects of Inward Prayer

Strangely, I had difficulty saying the vocal prayers I used to pray. As soon as I opened my lips to say them, the love of God seized me. I was swallowed up in a profound silence and inexpressible peace. I began again and again, but could not go on. I didn't know what to do. Within me there was a continual wordless prayer, just as it says in the Gospel—"If a man love me . . . my Father will love him, and we will come unto him, and make our abode with him" (John 14:23).

A few weeks after I received this interior gift of God's love, I went to a feast, which was my first opportunity to confess my sins. But I could not feel myself ready to confess! After sitting five hours in the church, I was so penetrated with a dart of pure love that I could not resolve the pain of my sins. So I surrendered myself to God and went home. I wrote a letter about this to the Franciscan, which he treasured so much he used it as a sermon.

I now stopped going to plays, dances, and parties. For two years I did not have my hair dressed. It became me, and my husband agreed. My only pleasure was to steal moments to be alone with God. I did not lose His presence, which was continually infused in me—not by efforts of my mind, but through a true union in the will, knowing by this experience that the soul is created to enjoy God.

I saw, O God, that Thou created the soul to enjoy its God. When the soul is docile and emptied of all its own, it wishes nothing but what Thou wilt.

Out of love for God, I searched out my faults. And divine love enlightened my heart and helped me scrutinize its secret springs to expose the smallest defects. If I was about to speak, something about the words I was to speak was instantly pointed out as wrong, and I was compelled to be silent. When a hint of pride or self-centeredness surfaced, I sensed an internal burning that pained me. It was like a dislocated joint that hurts until the bone is put in place. This pain was so severe that my soul would do anything to satisfy God for the fault.

My respect for the Cross increased. I tried to feel the utmost burden of my sin. The more my state of prayer deepened, the less I minded the heavy crosses of domestic life. I endured the insulting treatment of my husband and mother-in-law silently. This wasn't as difficult anymore because my interior life was so rich that my outward life could not hurt me. I involved myself in giving medicines to the sick and dressing their sores and wounds. At first, I could barely stand to do this. But in time I could endure the most offensive things. I did nothing of myself, but left myself to be governed by my Sovereign.

4

Opposition and Despair

My husband was not pleased with my newfound devotion. "You love God so much that you don't love me," he told me. He did not understand that marital love comes from the love the Lord forms in the heart. God gave me a purity of soul so that my husband sometimes said, "One sees plainly that you never lose the presence of God."

Restrictions and Confinement

These crosses would have seemed little if I'd had the freedom to pray and be alone, but I was once again forced to stay in my mother-in-law's room or at my husband's bedside at all times so they could monitor my prayer. I dared not leave. Sometimes I carried my work to the window pretending to need light to see better, when I really wanted a moment of quiet. They followed me to see if I prayed instead of working. When my husband and mother-in-law played cards, they watched to see if I turned toward the fire. Then they kept watch to see if I continued my work or shut my eyes. If they saw me close them, they swelled up in fury against me for hours.

To be agreeable, I often played cards with my husband. At such times I was even more inwardly attracted to God than if I had been to church! I could scarcely contain the fire which burned in my soul. The more others tried to suppress this fire, the more it gained strength.

When my husband went out (having some days of health), he marked my work to see if I progressed. If I did not, he assumed I'd lapsed into prayer. Sometimes he would leave and then immediately return to trap me. If he found me praying, he would fly into a rage. I asked him, "Sir, why does it matter what I do when you are absent, if I am attentive to you when you are present?" He insisted I not pray in his presence or his absence.

My mother-in-law also found fault with my going to church to say prayers. I would not go until my household duties were done, but she would tell my husband I left nothing in order. When I returned home, his violent rage fell on me. My explanations were called a pack of lies. My mother-in-law persuaded my husband to believe that if she did not take the care of the household, he would be ruined. I patiently tried to do my duty, but if I ordered anything without her, she complained that I showed her no respect. Then she would re-order the opposite. If I consulted her to find out her wishes, she said I forced her to take care of everything.

My inexperience in life caused me much of this trouble. I often gave them reasons to make me suffer. I see now that I should have viewed my captivity as God's will and made myself content with it.

My maid used my new devotion to taunt me since her insults did not. She began spying on me and telling my husband and mother-in-law whenever I went to Communion. Since my going to church upset them all, I stopped going so often and tried hard to pray to God in the temple of my heart.

O my God, the war they raised to hinder me from loving Thee only added to my love. While they strived to keep me from addressing Thee, Thou drew me into an inexpressible silence. The more they labored to separate me from Thee, the more closely Thou united me to Thyself.

My Priest's Opposition

My priest, who had declared me a saint before when I was so full of miseries, criticized me for placing my confidence in the Franciscan. The brothers in the priest's order preached publicly against me, saying I was under delusion.

My husband and mother-in-law, who till now had been indifferent about this priest, then joined him and ordered me to stop my inward prayer. I could not do this. So I tried to look as if I was not inwardly conversing with God, but they said it showed on my face. This pained my husband.

My priest tried to force me to stop from practicing inward prayer and from seeing Genevieve Granger, prioress of the nearby Benedictine convent. He urged my husband and mother-in-law to stop me from praying, so they began watching me from morning until night. My husband forced me to stay all day with my mother-in-law. (When I was younger, they kept me constantly in their presence because I supposedly had an evil spirit. Now, it was because I prayed too much.)

As I practiced inward prayer and detachment from the world, it seemed as if everyone ridiculed me in return. People entertained themselves with jokes of my piety. They could not bear that a woman, scarcely twenty years of age, should not be enchanted by the world's pleasures. My mother-in-law even ridiculed me for not doing many things that she would have been highly offended if I had done!

Turning Away From Prayer

These restrictions had an effect. I stopped finding vigor to keep up the inward prayer. My tendency toward pride showed itself again. I wished I were not so attractive and prayed that God would remove it.

Visiting in Paris, I did things I should not do. I allowed people to make over me. One day I took a walk in the public park not to enjoy the park but to show myself off. How did God show me my fault? By holding me so close that I couldn't think of anything but my faults and His displeasure. After this I was invited with some other ladies to a party, and I went. The affair was magnificent, but I was filled with bitterness. I could eat nothing and enjoy nothing. Oh, what tears!

Then as I walked to church, I met a poor man. I went to give him alms (donations to the poor), but he refused them. He spoke to me instead, saying it was not enough to avoid hell, but that the Lord required purity of me. His words penetrated my soul. When I arrived at the church, I fainted. I have never seen the man since.

O my Lord, with what strictness did Thou chide me. A useless glance was checked as a sin. My inadvertent faults cost me so many tears! Like a father tenderly forgiving a child who makes mistakes, Thou made me know Thy love

for me. The sweetness of Thy love after my falls caused me
pain. I regretted having departed from Thee.

Even though I was turning away, I still sought the God who had inflamed my heart. I called out to God. I saw how I'd sullied God's efforts in me, so I left Paris and returned quickly to the country house. The pain I felt after such faults devoured me like fire, and they did not cease until the fault was charred and the soul purified. "Oh my Father," said I, "Nothing else, besides Thee, can give solid pleasure."

Renewal and Spiritual Marriage

On my return, I told Mother Granger of my inner turmoil. She encouraged me to follow my convictions—even to dress more modestly. I felt such agony for having abused God's grace. I wished to hide myself in a cave or be confined in a dreary prison rather than enjoy freedom which only tripped me up. My heart was divided between God and my pride.

It was at this point I acknowledged that God had made an everlasting marriage union with me. To this union, God brought goodness, mercy, and love. I brought with me weakness, sin, and misery. I asked God to make me do what was right so I couldn't displease Him.

After that, each time my vanity showed itself, I quickly returned to God. Instead of scolding me, God received me with open arms, reminding me of His love. At times I wished He would scold me instead. I was stung to the quick for offending Him when He showered grace on me.

Thou has treated me as a king who marries a poor
slave, forgets her slavery, gives her what she needs to be

38

beautiful, and pardons her faults and selfish qualities. My poverty has become my riches, and in my extreme weakness, I have found strength.

Sickness and Death

My husband was overcome with gout, and then my older son and daughter became ill with smallpox. I was advised to leave the house and take my younger son to keep us from getting it. My father offered to take us, but my mother-in-law would not allow it. Many people in the town begged her to let us go so we would not be exposed to smallpox. Then they started in on me, thinking I was unwilling to go. (I had not admitted it was she who was against it.) I thought God must be speaking through her resistance, so I decided to sacrifice myself to do whatever God ordained. I was fearful, especially for my younger son.

At first I began to shiver and experience stomach pain, and then my lungs became inflamed. Finally I was so weak I couldn't open my mouth. My mother-in-law's physician was not in town, so she called in another who said I must be bled. She did not agree, so she sent the physician away. I enjoyed peace within, looking for life or death from the hand of God.

A doctor I knew passed by our house and asked about me. When he found out I was ill, he came to see me. The smallpox was so thick that my nose was black. He thought it was gangrene and that my nose might fall off! My eyes were like two coals. He was so frightened he went to my mother-in-law and insisted I be bled, but she opposed it. He flew into a rage at seeing me left without medical care and admonished her severely.

He then came to me and said, "If you want, I will bleed you, which will save your life." I held my swelled arm out to him, and he bled me. My mother-in-law threw a fit, but the smallpox came out immediately. He ordered that I should be bled again in the evening, but she would not allow it. Because I feared my mother-in-law, I did not oppose her.

The blackness and swelling of my nose grew worse as my eyes were inflamed. I could not open my eyes from the pain, yet I couldn't shut them because they were full of smallpox. For three weeks I could not sleep. My throat, palate, and gums were filled with pocks, so I couldn't swallow broth without severe pain. My body looked leprous. People who visited me said they'd never seen such a shocking spectacle.

My younger son, who was four years of age,[6] became sick the same day as myself and died. This blow struck me to the heart, but I offered him up, saying as Job did, "The Lord gave, and the Lord hath taken away; blessed be the name of the Lord" (Job 1:21). The spirit of sacrifice possessed me so strongly that I never shed a tear, although I loved this child tenderly. The doctor told me he had not placed a tombstone upon his grave because my little girl could not survive him two days. And my eldest son was not yet out of danger, so I saw myself stripped of all my children at once, my husband indisposed, and myself extremely ill.

At last my mother-in-law's physician arrived. When he saw the inflammation in my eyes, he bled me several times. Because my arms were so swollen, the doctor had to push the lance deeply into my arm. At that late date, the bleeding only weakened me.

---

[6] Upham, p. 81.

But my little girl did survive, and my older son got better, too. When he came into my room, I was surprised that his face, which had been so handsome, had become full of furrows, like a rugged piece of earth.

I became curious about my appearance and asked for a mirror. I saw that God had given me what I asked for, taking away my beauty. I was then given ointment to heal my complexion and fill up the crevices of the smallpox. I started to use it since I had seen wonderful results from it on others, but then I stopped. I was thankful God had taken away my source of pride. A voice in my heart said, "If I wanted you pretty, I would have left you that way." So I went out into the air, which made the pitting worse. I wanted to expose my pock-marked face in the street when the redness of the smallpox was at its worst to let my humiliation win over my pride in my appearance.

When my husband saw that I had lost my beauty (which he prized) at the young age of twenty-two, he grew more receptive to others' criticism of me. As a result, they spoke more boldly and more frequently against me.

Only Thou, O my God, did not change. Thou doubled my interior graces in proportion as my exterior crosses were expanded.

5

Clinging to God in the Midst of Crosses

My smallpox and my younger son's death brought no change to my household circumstances. When my husband and mother-in-law quarreled, they favored me and complained to me about each other. And though I could have used these things to my advantage, I did not. I never told the one what the other had said. Indeed, I worked to reconcile them. I said good things of the one to the other, which made them friends again. I knew I would pay dearly for their reunion because then they'd join up against me.

The only rest I found was in the love of God. Friends told me to pretend to be sick to get rest from my household duties, but I did not. The love of God so closely possessed me that it would not allow me to seek relief by a single word or an exasperated look.

How bitter and grievous, O my God, would such a life be were it not for Thee! Thou has sweetened life for me.

Household Crosses

Mother Granger was a help. I concealed neither my sins nor my pains from her. She cautioned me not to be too rigorous on myself. One day I ran off to Mother Granger, but it was discovered and cost me the rage of my husband and mother-in-law. Sending Mother Granger letters was difficult because my mother-in-law often hid in a little passageway by the door, asking anyone who went out if I'd given them letters to carry. I did not want to lie or ask the footman to lie. If I walked to the monastery to see her, I carried shoes to change into so my mother-in-law would not see the dirt on my shoes when I returned and guess I'd walked somewhere. Those who attended me were ordered to tell her every place I went. If they didn't do so, they were corrected or discharged.

The most difficult cross was their turning my older son, Armand, against me. They taught him such contempt for me that he scolded me as they did. I hurt inside every time I saw him. If I sat in my room with friends, they sent him to listen to what we said. Since they liked his spying, he invented a hundred things to tell them. If I caught him in a lie, he would chide me, saying, "My grandmother says you have been a greater liar than I." I answered, "Therefore, I know what a vice lying is and how difficult it is to stop it."

One day my son went to see my father and spoke against me as he did to his grandmother, but it was not met with the same reward. It pushed my father to tears. He came to our house and asked them to correct my son, which they promised to do. I grieved that they did not, but Mother Granger said that since I could not change it, I would be better off accepting it.

So in the midst of these crosses, I once again practiced continual prayer. I sensed the presence of God so much that there seemed to be more of God in me than myself in me. God's presence seemed powerful, penetrating—irresistible. At times, however, I did not pray and felt the pain of His absence. I wondered if God's presence would ever return again. I thought this lack was my fault, and that upset me. I did not know it was a necessary phase through which I needed to pass, or I would not have been so troubled.

This inward prayer gave me a great love for God with an unusual reliance on Him. I feared nothing—danger, thunders, spirits, or even death. It distracted me from myself and my interests. I was swallowed up in my desire to do God's will.

At this point, I decided that the greatest cross would be to be without these crosses. Every time the crosses stopped for a brief time, I saw that I had not used them well, missing out on advantages to my soul by not responding properly. I could not reconcile these two opposite things: to desire the crosses for their advantages; to bear them when they caused so much difficulty and pain.

Gradually, I understood that experiencing crosses was more profitable than living a life that abounded with blessing. Without crosses, the soul never dies to itself. Blessings lead to self-love, which is crafty and dangerous because of how it is woven into everything we do.

If Thou, O God, had spared the strokes of Thy hammer, I should never have been formed to be an instrument for Thy use. Some of Thy children, O God, can be faithful. As for me, I cannot. I owe all to Thee.

God's Coincidences

In the midst of these crosses, God seemed to show me special favors as I looked for His grace continually. We went into the country for a time because my husband supervised some building projects (which was at the heart of his great fortune[7]). Since I was allowed no time for prayer and was not allowed to get up until seven o'clock, I woke myself at four o'clock and knelt in my bed to pray. But this loss of rest was difficult. I was afraid I wouldn't wake up, so I woke myself up many times in the night. My eyes, still weak from the smallpox eight months before, became worse, and I fell asleep during my prayers anyway.

So I used my old method and got up early and walked to church a little less than a mile, which was difficult because of my weakness from the smallpox. God worked wonders, though, because my husband never awakened until after I returned. When the weather was cloudy, the servant girl I took with me feared I would be soaked with rain. I answered her with confidence, "God will assist us." We always reached the chapel without getting wet. While there, the rain fell hard, but as we returned, it ceased. Then, when we got home, it would begin again with fresh violence.

I could fill volumes with such "coincidences." At times, I wanted to pray when the chapel wasn't being served by a priest. I would go anyway, and a priest would be there! When I wanted to hear from Mother Granger, I often felt a strong urge to go to the door, and there I'd find a messenger with a letter from her.

---

7 Upham, pp. 18–19.

At the country house, I often went into the woods and caverns to pray. How many times God protected me there from beasts! At times, I knelt on snakes without realizing it, but they moved away without harming me. Once I happened to be alone in a wooded area where there was a mad bull, but he ran away. God's protection of me was so constant that I was astonished.

Helping Others

In these crosses, I not only enjoyed inward prayer, but also continued to enjoy doing acts of charity. I felt tender toward the poor and wished to supply their needs. Seeing them without so many things reproached me for the plenty I enjoyed. So I deprived myself to help them. The very best at my table was distributed to the poor. I found ways to give things away without letting myself be known. I arranged it so young girls could be taught to earn a livelihood, hoping that an income would keep them from throwing themselves away. Several were reclaimed from wayward living in this manner. I visited the sick, comforting them and making their beds. I made ointments, dressed their wounds, and buried their dead. My heart was open toward my fellow creatures in distress.

About nine months after my smallpox recovery, a priest came to me, Father La Combe, bringing a letter to me from my half brother,[8] Father de la Mothe, recommending him to me. I hesitated because I did not like making new acquaintances, but I feared offending my brother. We had a short conversation.

---

[8] In the manuscripts, she calls De la Mothe her brother, but Upham cites him as a half brother, p. 88.

When Father La Combe came again to our country house to visit my husband, the priest became ill and retired to the garden. My husband asked me to see if he needed anything. When I did, he told me he had noticed an inward presence of God in my countenance. I then explained to him the interior path of the soul, and this changed him into a quite another man—he told me this later. (Their conversation also created a crisis in his life, which caused him to choose to be wholly committed to God.[9])

A lady of very high rank among the nobility took a particular liking to me. She said I was pleasant, but also that there was something extraordinary about me. She asked me to go to a play with her, but I refused. I told her I never went to plays because of my husband's continual illness. She pressed me and said, "Don't let his sickness keep you from going out. You are too young to be confined with the sick like a nurse." So I told her about my desire to stay devoted to God and that plays distracted me from God. Although she had no reason to listen to me because I was younger, she was impressed by what I said and decided never to go to plays again.

This lady of high rank began to be touched with the sense of God. Once I joined another woman and her as they talked about religious books. I said almost nothing, being inwardly drawn to silence and somehow troubled by the conversation. The next day, the lady of rank said the Lord had touched her heart the previous day. I assumed it was by the other lady's words, but she said, "Your silence had something in it which penetrated my soul."

---

[9] Upham, p. 89.

As she became more thirsty for God, her affectionate husband died. This proved to be a severe cross, yet God poured His grace into her heart so that He soon became her sole master. She also lost most of her fortune and came to live twelve miles from our house on a small estate. She obtained my husband's consent to let me spend a week with her to console her. She understood a great deal, but was surprised at how I talked of deeper spiritual matters. God gave me the words to say to her, releasing a flood of grace into her soul in spite of my unworthiness.

At about this time, the doctor worried that I would lose an eye that had been damaged from smallpox. The gland at the corner of my eye was injured, and a sore developed from time to time between the nose and the eye, which gave me great pain. It swelled so much that I could not stand to use even a pillow.

Yet this agonizing time was precious to me for two reasons. First, I was left alone in bed where I could experience sweet retreat without interruption. And, second, it answered the desire I had for suffering so that I could experience the Cross of Christ.

> *It is Thou alone, O Crucified Saviour, who through Thy cross can help us die to self. Let others live in ease or pleasure, but for me, let my desires turn to the silent path of suffering. I want to be united to Thee. Let my senses, appetites, and will be dead to all else and wholly alive to Thee.*

6

Grief and Darkness

I obtained permission to go to Paris to get help for the sore near my eye, but I was also excited about spending ten days at an abbey twelve miles from Paris. The abbess there had a particular friendship for me. I no longer dreaded going to Paris as I had in the past. The throngs drew me into a deep reflection, and the noise of the streets increased my inward prayer.

One day while at the abbey, I awoke suddenly at four o'clock in the morning with a strong impression on my mind that my father was dead. My love for him gave me great sorrow. In the afternoon as I was with the abbess, I told her about my impression. I was so upset within I could hardly speak. Shortly after that, a messenger from my husband came saying that my father was ill. I said, "He is dead. I know it." As I found afterward, he was dead by that time.

Days of Grief

I took a coach at nine o'clock at night. Those at the abbey feared for my safety traveling by myself at night, but I felt it was my duty to go. I was so weak from the eye infection I could hardly keep myself in the seat of the coach. At dangerous places in the road, we were all forced to get out to lighten the load for a ways, yet I was in the care of Providence.

On my arrival at home at ten o'clock the next night, my husband informed me that my father had been buried because of the excessive heat. I had traveled ninety miles in a day, and I was very weak from having not eaten. I went to bed.

About two o'clock in the morning my husband left my chamber and returned crying with all his might, "My daughter is dead!" She was my only daughter, three years old,[10] whom I dearly loved. Her disposition was so sweet that a person could not help but love her. She had an extraordinary love for God. She could often be found in a corner at prayer. When we were alone and she saw my eyes closed, she would whisper, "Are you asleep?" Then she would cry out, "Ah no, you are praying to our dear Jesus." Dropping on her knees before me, she would pray, too. She was innocent as an angel, and her father doted on her. I looked upon her as my only consolation on earth. She had as much affection for me as her older brother had contempt.

She died of being bled at the improper time. But what shall I say? She died by the hands of Him who was pleased, for wise reasons of His own, to strip me of all. Yet I did not weep for my daughter or my father. I could only say, "You, O Lord, gave her to me. It pleases You to take her back again, for she was Yours."

I was twenty-three years old, and the only one of my three children left was the son of my sorrow, Armand. He fell ill to

---

10 Upham, p. 92.

the point of death, but was restored at the prayer of Mother Granger, who was now my only consolation besides God.

One day, being in great distress from inward and outward crosses, I went into my closet to grieve. I looked around for relief. A word, a sigh from someone else who also grieved, would have been some comfort. That was not granted me, yet love held me closely.

Oh, my dearest Lord! Thou gave my soul victorious support, which made it triumph. Thou, O my Shepherd, sometimes comforted me with Thy crook and Thy staff.

Moments of Happiness

As my husband's sicknesses increased, he decided to go to St. Reine. He wanted no one but me with him and said, "If others didn't speak to me against you, I would be more gentle and you would be more happy." My husband worried that he had no heirs except my firstborn son, who was sickly, so he prayed earnestly for more children. God granted his desire and gave me a second son.

Childbirth left me weak, which was good because people left me alone and I loved the time of retreat and of silence. It was then God took a new possession of me and left me not. I felt joy without interruption. Yet this brief happy time also prepared me for several years of hardship with no support.

Before I returned from St. Reine, I heard Mother Granger was dead. This was the most afflicting stroke I ever felt. I wished I'd been with her in death and received her last instructions. I also needed her in this trying season of briars and thorns; yet some months before, the Lord let me know that if I were somehow deprived of her, it would not be as damaging as it seemed.

> *O God whom I adore! It seems you wanted no one to guide me as Thou led me into the regions of darkness, where I must die totally to myself. It even seemed that after saving me from death, Thou led me by the hand in rugged paths. Who has known the mind of the Lord, or who has been His counselor? (Isa. 40:13, NIV).*

Conflict with My Brother

When my brother was married at Orleans, my husband showed him the courtesy of taking me to his marriage ceremony even though he was in poor health. Snow covered the roads so that our coach nearly overturned twelve or fifteen times. Far from appearing grateful for my husband's efforts, my brother quarreled with him more than ever without reason. I was the butt of both their resentments.

Then a certain person became determined to ruin my husband. He obtained a power to demand, in the name of the king's brother, 200,000 livres (a livre was worth a pound of silver), which he pretended that my brother and I owed him. My brother did not know how to resolve it and refused to talk about it. This made my husband so angry with me that he could not speak to me except in a fury. He gave me no details of the affair, and in the height of his rage he said he would separate himself from me and give me a small wage to live on.

On the day of the trial, after prayer, I went to the judges. In so doing, I was able to unravel the twists and turns of the affair.

The first judge was so surprised to see the truth of the matter that he advised me to speak to the other judges. God enabled me to present the truth clearly so that they thanked me for correcting the false information. My husband was pleased, but my brother was deeply offended. Nevertheless, the alarming matter ended without great harm.

My Dark Night of the Soul

About this time I fell into a state of emptiness that lasted nearly seven years. I struggled internally between two powers. I desired to please God, but I also felt a continual rising of self. I wondered how God could have given me such closeness to Him only to take it away.

I could no longer pray as before. Heaven seemed shut to me. Doing good, virtuous things no longer seemed easy. Nothing helped—not vows, promises, prayers, pilgrimages. Tears were my drink and sorrow was my food. It was as if an executioner within tortured me. Even in church I was not be at ease. Sermons made no sense to me.

Occasionally there was relief. My husband had built a chapel in the country nearby so I could go there to pray. During the dedication of this chapel, I felt myself caught up by God inwardly during the ceremony. I saw myself as a temple dedicated to Him for time and eternity. I thought, regarding myself and the chapel, *This temple will never be impure. In it, the praises of will be sung forever!* I went home thinking my prayer was granted, but the emptiness returned.

In this seven years of desolation, I understood what Nebuchadnezzar said about feeling so cast down he wanted to live among beasts (Dan. 4). Since then, I have discovered that when the prayer of the heart appears dry and barren, the prayer is not pointless. God gives what is best for us, though not what we most wish for. We are called to enjoy God Himself and not merely His gifts. Otherwise, we spend our lives running after little happy moments, feeding on them instead of God.

Another Death

In the midst of this desolation from God, my husband's sicknesses were continuous. No sooner had he recovered from one illness than he caught another. He suffered patiently, offering it to God. As his illness grew worse every day, he understood death was approaching and wished for an escape from his languishing life. He disliked eating, but I sometimes got him to take some food. I saw plainly he could not live long.

At this time, the maid who troubled me became compassionate. She would say, "Come visit my master now so your mother-in-law will stop speaking against you."

I pretended to be ignorant of their dislike of me, but he could not conceal his displeasure from me. He did not even want me to be near him. Because of his pain, I believe he was more susceptible to evil reports of me and became more angry with me. My mother-in-law created so much displeasure against me in his mind that I feared he would die hating me. She actually started to keep me away from him.

One day, she happened not to be with him, so I drew near his bed, knelt down, and said, "I beg your pardon if I have done things that displease you—I did not mean to." He appeared to be touched by this and said, "It is I who beg your pardon. I did not deserve you." After that, he was pleased to see me and even gave me advice about what I should do after his death.

I sent to Paris for the most skillful doctor, but when he arrived my husband was dead. I was not present when he died, for he had out of tenderness told me to go to sleep. No mortal could die in a more Christian state of mind or courage than he did.

The next day I entered my closet, in which was my divine spouse, the Lord Jesus Christ. I renewed my marriage contract with God and added to it a vow of chastity. After that I was filled with great joy, which was new to me from my long time of deep bitterness.

Life as a Widow

I was a widow at the age of twenty-seven. After twelve years and four months of a marriage filled with many crosses, I was exhausted. I had just given birth to my second daughter, Marie Jeanne[11] and then sat up with my husband twenty-four nights before his death. It took more than a year to recover from this fatigue.

I felt so dry and depressed I could hardly speak. The household around me said I must be in mortal sin, and I had nobody in the world to speak to. I had no guide, no friend, no counselor. I had lost all. Not only had God taken from me one person after another, but He also withdrew Himself. If I'd had only my eldest son, I would have put him in college and entered a convent, but I still had my young son and daughter born shortly before my husband's death.

---

[11] Her name is supplied by Upham, p. 468.

There was also my husband's wealth and huge estate to manage. I paid off the grants he had promised. I was ignorant of legal matters, but God supplied me with wisdom. I understood the business documents and took care of my affairs without anyone's assistance. Because my husband had been sick a long time, everything was in confusion, and I took an exact inventory of the documents of others that had been entrusted to him and returned them to their owners. This gained me the reputation of being a skillful woman.

Several persons involved in a legal dispute had asked my husband to settle it for them. There were twenty legal actions involved and twenty-two persons concerned who needed to settle differences. At my husband's death, I tried to return their legal documents, but they wouldn't take them. They begged me to help them and prevent their ruin. This was ridiculous, of course, but I decided to rely on the strength and wisdom of God. I secluded myself for thirty days to examine these affairs and then prepared an agreement, which they all signed with satisfaction. God alone did these things. After that, or even now, any talk of such things sounds like Arabic to me.

To my surprise, being a widow increased my crosses. My turbulent maid became more furious than ever. In our house she had amassed a good fortune, and I gave her an annuity for the remainder of her life for the way she had cared for my husband. She swelled with pride.

It turned out that in the nights she'd sat up with my husband, she'd begun drinking wine. As she grew aged and weak, a little wine affected her a great deal. I tried to hide this from others, but it could not be concealed. I spoke of it to her priest in order that he might try to gently help her, but instead she became enraged at me. My mother-in-law, who spoke vehemently against drinking, joined her in reproaching me. Whenever company came, this strange creature would cry out that I had caused her to be damned by God.

God somehow gave me endless patience. I answered her passionate accusations with mildness and charity, showing her my affection. If any other maid came to wait on me, this turbulent one would drive the other back in a rage. I waited for her then, and when she came, she chided me loudly. When she did not come, I did without.

As I ceased my activities—not seeing the poor, not going to church, not practicing inward prayer—I became colder toward God. All this destroyed me in my own eyes. Important gentlemen made proposals for me (even those above me in rank) during this depth of desolation. At first, I thought that accepting a proposal might draw me out of the distress I was in.

> *But even if a king had presented himself to me, I would have refused him with pleasure, to show Thee, O my God, that with all my miseries I was resolved to be Thine alone. If Thou would not accept me, I should at least be faithful to Thee to the utmost of my power.*

Then I fell ill for five or six weeks so that I could not eat or drink. A spoonful of broth made me pass out. My voice was so faint that when people put their ears to my mouth, they could scarcely distinguish my words. I could not see any hope of salvation, and I was willing to die. All my troubles, combined with the loss of my reputation (which was not as marred as I feared), rendered me unable to eat. Reading spiritual books only enlarged my distance from God. How could God bear my cliquishness, pretended courtesy, and pointless conversations? My self-love made me indulge in them, but how was I to find God again?

7

Reawakening to God

During this time of death and desolation, I went on business to the town where my mother-in-law's relatives lived. When I had visited before, they treated me with courtesy, presenting me proudly to friends. Now they shunned me, saying they were taking revenge on me for how I made my mother-in-law suffer.

So when I returned home, I spoke plainly to my mother-in-law. If she truly believed I'd treated her ill, I would leave her household to avoid giving her more pain. She answered coldly, "Do what you will. I said nothing about you to anyone."

So I kept trying to do right by her. When I went to the country house to rest, she complained I left her alone. If I asked her to come with me, she would not. If I didn't ask her, she said I didn't want her to go. One time I heard she was upset that I'd gone to the country, so I returned to town only to find she would not see me or speak to me. I pretended not to notice this and spoke to her anyway, but she turned her head away. While in the country, I often sent her my coach, asking her to come and spend the day with me. She sent it back empty. Then, if I didn't send it for a few days, she complained about it.

When we were together on Christmas Day, I said to her, "My mother, on this day the King of Peace was born to bring peace. I beg peace of you in His name." I think that touched her, though she said nothing.

One of her friends urged me not to leave and spoke to her for me. She told him she would not push me out but if I went she would not stop me.

He asked me to apologize to her once more, even though my apologies seemed to upset her more. Upon his insistence, he and I went to her room where I begged her pardon. I said I'd never intended to offend her. She replied, "I am not a person who is easily offended. I have no other complaint against you except that you don't love me and wish me dead." I replied that these thoughts were far from my heart and I wished her a long life. We embraced and it was left in this puzzling state.

I believe my mother-in-law had a good heart, but a volatile temperament. She had good qualities, and her faults were only those often found in persons who do not practice prayer. Perhaps I caused her crosses without intending to, and she did so to me without knowing it.

Living on My Own

I looked for places to live, but I had been so isolated in my widowhood that I had no idea where to go. I felt lost. I feared moving out in the middle of winter with my children and my daughters' nurse. I looked, but there was no house empty in the town, so the Benedictines offered me an apartment in theirs. During this time my inner misery continued. I did not go on outings or enjoy parties. I wanted to see and know nothing but

Jesus Christ. My prayer closet was my only diversion. Even when the queen, who lived nearby and whom I'd always hoped to meet was passing by, I did not look out my window.

About eight or ten days before St. Magdalene's Day, (July 22[12]), 1680, I wrote to Father La Combe and asked him to pray for me. He prayed for me on St. Magdalene's Day, and he heard a "voice" say three times very powerfully: "You shall both dwell together." He was surprised, since he'd never received interior words before.

I believe, O my God, that these words have been verified in the way he and I have experienced similar crucifying events and have allowed Thyself to be our dwelling.

My Spirit Awakening

On that happy Magdalene's Day, my soul was delivered from its pains. I sensed new life when I received that letter from Father La Combe—like a person raised from the dead yet still bound in grave clothes. I was set free on that day. God, whom I thought I had lost forever, returned to me with unspeakable magnificence and purity. As I viewed my previous troubles, I thought of the apostle Paul's words: "The sufferings of this present time are not worthy to be compared with the glory which shall be revealed in us" (Rom. 8:18).

It was then, O God, I found in Thee new advantages. All I had enjoyed before was only a peace, a gift of God, but now I received and possessed the God of peace.

---

12 Upham, p. 44.

As I entered a newness of life toward the end of nearly seven years of emptiness, our Lord showed me that the exterior crosses came from Him and that I shouldn't resent the persons who treated me harshly. On the contrary, I felt compassion for them and was sorry for the trouble I innocently caused them. I saw that these persons feared the Lord too much to have plagued me as they did on their own. God's hand must have been in it. It is hard to imagine the tenderness God gave me for them and the desire I had to give them every sort of advantage.

Once again, I was ready to do good. Whenever a self-absorbed thought presented itself, I rejected it as if I'd drawn a curtain in front of it. I marveled at the clearness of my mind and the purity of my whole heart.

Oh, my Lord, Thou can take the weak and the wretched to do Thy works that Thou may have all the glory. If Thou should take famous or talented persons, they might think highly of themselves, but if Thou take me, it will be obvious that thou alone are the Author of whatever good shall be done.

I continued quiet in my spirit, leaving all to God, being satisfied that if He wanted something of me He would furnish me with the means of performing it. I held myself in readiness to do as He asked. In losing all God's gifts to me (father, husband, children, pleasing appearance) with all their supports, I found the Giver. I pondered how we pass the time treasuring God's gifts and thinking ourselves happy. We must not stop there, short of true rest, but go forward to God Himself—through the loss of those cherished gifts.

What happiness I tasted in my solitude and with my little family, where nothing interrupted my tranquility! As I was living in the country and my children were in good hands, I withdrew into the woods. I passed as many days of happiness as I had had months of sorrow.

> *Thou, O my God, dealt with me as Thou did with Thy servant Job, returning double for all Thou had taken, and delivering me from all my crosses.*

Suddenly, others found me pleasing. Even my mother-in-law declared she was satisfied with me, yet I did nothing differently. Those who had cut me down now praised me. I remained in an entire peace, without as well as within.

It seemed to me that my soul became like New Jerusalem, where there is no more sorrow. I felt a complete indifference to everything on earth because my union with the will of God was so great that my own will seemed entirely lost. I desired nothing beyond what I had and was content with whatever happened. If a servant asked me, "Will you have this, or that?" I could not answer. Smaller matters quite disappeared, a higher power having filled their place.

It seemed as if I had passed into God, to become part of Him—even as a drop of water cast into the sea becomes part of it. Oh, union of unity, how strong is a soul that is become lost in its God! I remain hid with Christ in God (Col. 3:3).

A Missionary Trip?

During the time of my dark night of the soul, the city of Geneva came to mind (a Protestant stronghold Louis XIV had tried to convert by military force,[13] located in present-day Switzerland). *What?* I wondered. *Shall I desert God not only in my spiritual life but also my doctrine?* How could I ponder leaving the church for which I'd gladly have martyred myself?

I was afraid for my soul, but then I received a letter from that good Father La Combe about his concern that the people of Geneva acquire a knowledge of God. This restored peace and calmness to my mind because he was a person of faith. Afterward, in a dream, a woman appeared from heaven to tell me that God had called me to Geneva.

After my reawakening to God, I received another letter from Father La Combe, in which he wrote that God had revealed to him that He had great designs for me. "Whatever it might be, it is all the same to me," I said to myself. I still had the souls of Geneva at heart, but said nothing about it to anyone, waiting for God to make known His all powerful will. I also said nothing because I feared some strategy of the devil was concealed in it that would steal me out of my joy in God. Yet I saw how my former misery outfitted me for the designs of God, whatever they might be.

Confirmation

At this time, I had business in Paris, so while there, I entered a church to pray. Even though I said nothing to the priest there, he surprised me by saying, "I don't know who you are or anything about you, but I feel a strong inward urge to tell

---

13 John W. Cowart. *People Whose Faith Got Them into Trouble* (Downers Grove, IL: InterVarsity Press, 1990), p. 71.

you to do what the Lord has made known to you. I have nothing else to say."

I answered him, "I am a widow with little children. What else could God require of me but to take proper care of them and educate them?" He replied, "If God requires something of you, nothing in this world will hinder you from doing His will." This surprised me, but I told him nothing about Geneva. Within myself, I became contrite, eager to do as God directed, letting no separation come between my will and God's will in me.

In this state of restful waiting, I lived in tranquility with my family until one of my friends had a desire to go on a mission to Siam (present-day Thailand). He lived sixty miles from my house, and as he got ready to go, he found himself stopped by an impulse to come and speak to me. At first, he was reluctant to tell me this, but when he did, I told him about my idea of going to Geneva and the dream I'd had about it. Then I said, "God sent you to give me advice." After three days of prayer and pondering, he told me he believed I was to go to Geneva, but to be sure of it, I should see the Bishop of Geneva. If he approved of my design, it would be a sign that it was from the Lord. If not, I must drop it.

I agreed with my friend, and he offered to speak to the bishop for me and report back. Yet my friend was older, so we deliberated how he should transport himself on so long a journey. At that moment, two travelers came along and told us the Bishop of Geneva was in Paris. What extraordinary providence!

My friend advised me to write to Father La Combe and ask for his prayers. He then went to Paris and spoke to the

Bishop of Geneva, and having reason to go to Paris, I came later and spoke to the bishop also.

I told the bishop I wanted to go to Geneva and set up an establishment for people willing to serve God and give themselves to Him without reserve. The bishop approved of my plan and gave his permission for me to go. He pointed me toward a group, the New Catholics, who were establishing themselves in Gex, a city in easternmost France near Geneva.

I went to see the prioress of the New Catholics at Paris, and she assured me she would like to join me in my missionary endeavor. Because I considered her to be a great servant of God, this confirmed my mission.

I could see God using the prioress because of her virtue and me because of my wealth and substance. I also saw that the more I was nothing, the more fit I was for His designs. Yet I was also afraid of being too hasty and missing God's will.

More Confirmation

I'd written the Franciscan who had helped me so much and asked for his prayers. He finally replied that the Lord had shown him that He required me at Geneva. I asked if perhaps the Lord desired that I donate money to establish an institution there, but he replied that the Lord had revealed to him that He wanted me, not my worldly substance.

At the same time I received a letter from Father La Combe, saying that the Lord had given his colleagues and him a certainty that He wanted me at Geneva. I was surprised to receive two letters exactly alike at the same time from two persons living so far from each other—more than four hundred and fifty miles.

I left myself in the hands of God, resolved not to take any step, either to make the thing succeed or to hinder it, but to move as He should be pleased to direct me. I also had mysterious dreams, which hinted at great crosses, yet I submitted my heart to do whatever pleased God.

In one of my dreams, I was going about my business when I saw a little animal that appeared to be dead. (I understood this animal represented the envy of some persons, but their envy seemed to be dead.) I picked up the animal, but it tried to bite me so I dropped it. My fingers were then filled with sharp-pointed needles. I asked a passerby to take them out, but he pushed them deeper in and left me that way. Then a charitable priest picked up this animal with a pair of animal claws. (I can still remember the face of that priest though I have never seen him. I believe I shall before I die.) As the priest held the animal, the sharp needles fell off my fingers.

I was also surprised to receive letters from several godly persons who, although they knew nothing of my plans, spoke of my going forth in the service of God, and some of them mentioned Geneva. One of them hinted that I would be persecuted there, and another said I would be eyes to the blind, feet to the lame, and arms to the maimed.

Reconciliation

While God appointed me to forsake all things, God also made my ties to them stronger. My own mother could not have been more affectionate than my mother-in-law was. She said she had "respect for my goodness."

I believe her attitude was largely due to hearing that three persons had offered marriage proposals, but I had refused them even though their fortune and rank were superior to mine. (This left the fortune and estate intact.) I think she was relieved that I did not take revenge on her scoldings by marrying with great honor and keeping my children from her. So she now was tender to me.

Then I fell extremely ill. During this illness, my mother-in-law never left my bedside, and her tears proved the sincerity of her affection. I was very much affected by this and felt I loved her as my true mother. How, then, could I leave her now, she being so far advanced in age? The maid who had plagued me also became my friend. She praised me continually, talking with respect about my character. She asked forgiveness for all she had made me suffer. So with my plans to leave, I accomplished what did not happen when I had no plans but to remain at home.

I set everything in order. I loved my children so much and felt such pain at leaving them, but saw I had to surrender all to God to follow His will. I believed God would furnish the necessary means to educate my children. The Lord alone was my guide.

8

Launching Out on My Mission

Though I had doubts about my missionary endeavor before I left, I never doubted its being God's will after I left. What concerned me most was my children, especially my younger son. I left him with my mother-in-law, and I took my daughter, Marie Jeanne, with me, hoping I was not risking her education. My "sacred marriage" to God forced me give up all, to follow my Spouse wherever He called me. People, however, judge things by success and have criticized my calling, putting it down as error, illusion, and imagination. The crosses I've suffered since (of which the imprisonment I now endure is one) have confirmed in me the truth and validity of my calling.

My only dilemma was whether I should join the New Catholics. Father La Combe wrote but did not tell me whether I ought to join them or not. Thus it was God alone, who orders everything, to whom I surrendered myself without reserve. And that hindered me from joining them.

Before I heard of the New Catholics going to Gex, my idea had been to rent a room in Geneva and avoid announcing my mission. I planned to use ointments to heal wounds and win them over by charity. If I had followed this impulse, things would have succeeded better. But I thought I ought to follow the sentiments of the bishop rather than my own. Now I see that God's design was to use my desire to go to Geneva to allow me to guide souls wherever I went, not to do good works in Geneva.

Even now, O God, I pray for the souls of that city to give themselves to Thee without reserve—by a way known only to Thee.

I was seized with fear that joining the New Catholics was not God's plan, but I wrote to Sister Garnier to get a contract drawn up according to my first mission. God permitted me to commit this error, to make me more aware of His protection over me. Father La Combe has since told me he had a strong impulse to write to me advising me not to join the New Catholics, as he did not believe this was God's will for me, but he omitted doing it.

Concealing my doubts, I went to the New Catholics at Paris. I gave them all the money I had, glad to be poor after the example of Jesus Christ. Of the nine thousand livres I had (a livre was equal to a pound of silver), I lent them six thousand. (This six thousand was returned to my children.) The rest I gave to the sisters traveling with us, paying for their expenses to Gex and purchasing furniture for them.

I traveled with the sisters by boat, and we arrived at Annecy (a French town south of Geneva) on St. Magdalene's Eve, 1681. Just off the boat, I met a poor man asking alms, and having nothing else, I gave him the buttons from my sleeves.

On St. Magdalene's Day, the Bishop of Geneva performed a service for us, and I renewed my spiritual marriage with my

Redeemer, as I did every year on this day. We left Annecy and went to Geneva the next day, where I prayed for the conversion of that great people. That evening we arrived late at Gex, where we found only bare walls. The Bishop of Geneva had assured me that the house was furnished, as he believed it was. We lodged at the house of the Sisters of Charity, who were so kind as to give us their beds.

As people in France slowly learned I had gone, they reacted. My half brother, Father de la Mothe, wrote to me that learned, influential people in Paris disapproved of my action. To alarm me still more, he informed me that my mother-in-law, who was caring for my younger son, was in a "second childhood" and unable to care for him. This, however, proved false.

I answered these fearful letters as the Spirit dictated. My answers were accepted, and the violent accusations changed to applause. Father de la Mothe seemed to respect me for a time, but his disapproval returned. Self-interest took hold of him, he being disappointed that I would now be unable to set aside a portion of my fortune for a pension he expected from me. Sister Garnier changed and declared against me as well.

I ate and slept little in Gex. The food given to us was putrid and full of worms because of the heat. Food I would once have abhorred now became my daily meals. All this seemed easy to accept. In God I found everything that I had given up for Him. I was able to do things that astonished me as well as others, yet I knew I had meager capabilities. When Jesus Christ, the Eternal Wisdom, is formed in the soul, the soul finds in Him all the good things it needs.

My daughter, Marie Jeanne, had lost too much weight, and I wept in secret for her. Finally, I decided to take her to a convent at Thonon[14] (a city on Lake Geneva in present-day Switzerland). When I suggested this, the New Catholic sisters opposed it strongly, seeming hard hearted and ungrateful. But my daughter was a skeleton! I worried that I had recklessly sacrificed this child. I wrote to Father La Combe, asking him to visit so he could advise me. I could not keep her there any longer in good conscience.

Tending to My Daughter

Father La Combe came quickly and told me of some extraordinary experiences he'd had in God. At first I suspected he was having illusions and flattering himself, but I also saw a genuine humility. Far from being elevated by his learning and profound gifts, no person could have a lower opinion of himself than he had. The grace that flowed from him reassured me.

Father La Combe agreed it would be best to take Marie Jeanne to Thonon. I also told him how I disliked the New Catholics' manner of life, and he told me he didn't think I was compatible with them. He warned me not to talk to them about my inward path of faith. If I did, I could expect persecution from them. He advised me to come back to Gex after my trip to Thonon and stay free from attachments until God made known to me how he would use me.

So I took my little daughter to the Ursuline Sisters at Thonon, but I was disappointed to find they already had other little girls boarding there who had destructive habits. What

---

14 The manuscript says Tonon, but I suspected it was present day Thonon-les-Bains, on the shores of Lake Geneva. T.C. Upham confirms this, p. 87.

would happen if I left her there with them? If I had left her back in France, she would have become a fine lady with a proper education. With her natural disposition and fine qualities, she would have had many marriage proposals. To take her back to Gex would mean she would never be fit for anything—if indeed she recovered physically. Could God be asking me to sacrifice this sweet, godly child?

All my tenderness for her was awakened, and I could not be her destroyer. I saw how Hagar must have suffered when she took her son Ishmael to the desert so she wouldn't see him perish. I wondered if God was purifying me from human attachments. I decided to leave her at the convent in Thonon, and in a short time she recovered.

My Purpose Revealed to Me

I had already begun to awaken regularly at midnight to pray, often with these words in my mind, "I come... to do Thy will, O God" (Heb. 10:7). These words were conveyed with the most pure, penetrating, and powerful communication of grace that I had ever experienced. I feared death no more. Often I continued on my knees in prayer, from midnight till four o'clock in the morning, in a sweet intercourse with God.

At times I needed rest, so God did not awaken me, but even in my sleep I felt a consciousness of God. In the years since, I have had only half-sleep, always conscious of God. In these nightly vigils, the Lord made known to me that He designed me to be a mother of many people—people who would be simple and childlike. Others took these disclosures literally and thought I should head an institution or congregation, but it appeared to me that God wanted me to win persons over to Him and to mother them through His goodness. In the process, I would bring them to walk in the way He leads. I shall show you how this happened.

Sometime after my arrival at Gex, the Bishop of Geneva came to see us. He was so convinced of God's hand on me that he opened his heart to me, confessing his faults and problems. He declared the truth of everything I said. (It was, however, the Spirit of truth that inspired me to speak, without which I would be a simpleton.)

Yet I found the bishop listened and accepted the words of everyone as truth, even when they spoke for self-seeking reasons. He gave in to whomever he was with. This kept him from doing the good he otherwise might have done.

After I spoke to the bishop, he appointed Father La Combe to be my spiritual director. I was glad because this enlightened man of God understood the inward path and had a gift for pacifying souls. Just then, I fell into a violent, painful sickness. The doctors said I was in great danger, yet the sisters of the house didn't take it seriously. Their administrator would not give me money for medicines I needed. I did not have a penny to help myself with because I'd given it all to them. They did write Father La Combe, asking him to come. He responded by walking on foot all night. (He always traveled this way to imitate our Lord Jesus Christ.)

When Father La Combe prayed and laid his hand on my head, I was cured. When my relatives in Paris heard of this miraculous cure through Father La Combe, they told other influential people who then wrote to me and donated money. They talked of printing an account of my sacrifice of wealth and my sudden recovery from illness. I don't know what came of that, but such is the petulance of people. Their applause provided a strange prelude for the strange condemnation that would come.

On Retreat

The sisters at Gex then advised me to return to my daughter in Thonon, and Father La Combe returned with me. After seeing her so well, I went into a retreat for twelve days. Here I made vows of chastity, poverty, and obedience, promising to obey the will of God and the church and to honor Jesus Christ. I felt immersed in God on this retreat. I found that the trying time of joining the sisters purified my soul instead of tainting it. I possessed God so immensely that my thoughts and desires were clean and without selfish motives. My imagination, so restless before, troubled me no more. My will, dead to its own appetites, was numb to human preferences. It was as if my soul began partaking of the qualities of her Spouse.

I found that the more my spirit was lost in its Sovereign, the more and more I was attracted to God Himself. This produces an unusual innocence, not understood by those who still live for themselves.

The joy that a soul possesses in Thee, O God, is so great that it experiences the truth of those words: "Your joy no man shall take from you" (John 16:22). It is as the soul were plunged in a river of peace. The soul is then so passive, so willing to receive from Thy hand either good or evil without selfish emotion.

9

Persecution Begins

I would prefer to suppress what I am about to write because people don't often comprehend God's hand in negative circumstances, but I have been instructed to omit nothing.

After I arrived back in Gex from Thonon, my relatives wrote to me, suggesting I give up the guardianship of my children and sign my fortune over to them, reserving an annuity for myself. They proposed this out of self-interest, but I did not mind. The document I signed also included scandalous clauses saying that if my children died, my relatives would inherit my estate instead of me. (I did not realize this; I had no one to advise me.) Yet it seemed to me that I could now be like Jesus Christ—poor, naked, and stripped of all.

At this time the devil began to oppose me openly. One night, to my surprise, something monstrous and frightful presented itself—a face in a glimmering bluish light. My soul rested calmly, and it appeared no more. As I arose at midnight to pray, I heard frightful noises in my chamber. My bed often shook for a quarter of an hour at a time, and the curtain sashes tore apart. During this turbulent time, I arose every morning and lit my wax candle, which I kept in my room because I had been assigned the role of waking the sisters and that of sacristan (caretaker of the communion vessels and custodian of the house). I would see curtain sashes torn, yet I felt no fear. I used my light to look over the room when the noise was loudest. As the Enemy saw that I was afraid of nothing, he suddenly stopped and attacked me no more in person. But he stirred up people against me, which succeeded much better. For he found people who thought it was wise to injure me.

Priestly Persecution

The noises in my chamber ended as the persecutions of a priest with great authority began. He had been having intimate conversations with one of the sisters at Gex. At first he persuaded her to dislike me, knowing that if she trusted me, I would advise her not to allow his frequent visits. She had planned to take a retreat with him as her director (which he wanted, so he could make advances toward her), but I urged her to wait until the new spiritual director for our house (Father La Combe) came, and she agreed.

I talked to her about inward prayer and drew her into this practice. Our Lord blessed her in this, and she gave her entire heart to God. As a result, she became more guarded toward this priest, which vexed him. He became enraged at both Father La Combe and me. He spoke with contempt about me to others, but I did not acknowledge it.

This slandering priest won over the house administrator and the prioress of the sisters at Gex. They created trouble with the two maids I had brought with me (because I was not physically strong since birth and even more so since the small-pox). The community needed one of them for their cook and needed the other to attend the door, so I gave them up, assuming they would be allowed to help me sometimes. I paid their salary out of my annuity. Yet the sisters would not permit either of my maid servants to help me. By my office of sacristan, I was obliged to sweep the church, which was large, and they would not let anyone help me. Several times I became faint while sweeping and sat down to rest in a corner. I begged them to have the stronger country girls sweep, and they finally consented.

What most embarrassed me was that I had never washed garments and I was now obliged to wash the communion linen. I took one of my maids to help me because I did up the linen awkwardly the first time. These sisters pulled her out of my chamber by her arms, telling her she should do her own work. I let it quietly pass without objecting.

In the meantime, the sister I'd taught about inward prayer grew closer to God and to me. This irritated the priest. He went directly to the Bishop of Geneva, who until this time had shown respect and kindness toward me, and persuaded him to force me to donate my entire annual income to the house the New Catholics were establishing at Gex. He suggested that I could be bribed into doing this by being named prioress. (This priest had gained such influence over the bishop that the people nicknamed him "the little bishop.")

That's when the priest then began targeting me in earnest. He intercepted all my letters so I wouldn't hear about the gossip he was spreading about me to my friends in France. When I was asked to be the prioress, I told them I could not because I had not passed through the two-year novitiate (beginners' period). When I had finished that period, I would see how God inspired me. The current prioress replied tartly that if I was planning to leave them, it would be best for me to do it immediately. But I didn't offer to leave.

I saw the sky gradually thickening and storms gathering on every side. The prioress then used a milder tone, pretending to respect me and asking me if she could go with me to Geneva to serve God. At this point, I let her know I was not likely to join the New Catholics because they did not seem upright in everything. She indicated that she did not consent to certain procedures either, but she allowed them because they were necessary to give the house credibility and to draw donations from Paris. I insisted that if we walked uprightly, God would never fail us. God would even do miracles for us.

Soon after this, Father La Combe came to give retreats. The prioress asked permission to go to Geneva with me, but he answered in his usual straightforward way: "Our Lord has made known to me that you shall never be established at Geneva." At this she became enraged against both him and me. She, that priest, and the house administrator conspired to force me either to join the New Catholics or to leave. Then the prioress died.

The persecutions were very hard on my maids. I had already sent one home because the sisters at Gex had worn her out. Then the other wanted to go back and began complaining. She criticized me for leaving such a good life behind—how could I have come to Gex, this good-for-nothing place? It hurt me to hear her agitation and the clamor of her tongue.

Out to Get Father La Combe

Hoping to ensnare Father La Combe, the priest asked him to preach. Afterward, the priest claimed the sermon had been full of errors. He inserted eight new statements into Father La Combe's sermon, arranging them to appear malicious. Then he sent a copy of the sermon to Rome to be examined by the Inquisition. To his surprise, Rome pronounced the sermon good. That vexed him so that he berated Father La Combe with the most offensive terms.

After this treatment, Father La Combe humbly offered to deliver any letters the priest might have for the bishop since he was going to see him in Geneva. The priest asked him to wait a few minutes while he wrote.

Father La Combe waited more than three hours without hearing from the priest and, upon checking, discovered the priest had sent a servant on horseback, ordered to go full speed, to see the bishop before Father La Combe. It was obvious he had done this to sway the bishop against him. Father La Combe then set off and found the bishop preoccupied and upset. He relayed their conversation to me:

Bishop: You must persuade this lady to give what she has to the New Catholics. Then make her the prioress of the sisters there.

Father La Combe: My lord, you know she has no wish to join them. She has offered to stay with the sisters as a boarder only. If they are willing to keep her, she'll remain. If not, she will go to a convent unless God leads her otherwise.

Bishop: I know that. But she is very obedient and will join the New Catholics if you order her to.

Father: Because she is so obedient, my lord, one ought to be cautious in commanding her to do anything. How can I persuade this lady, who has given up her wealth and kept only a pittance for herself, to give up the rest of her money to a house which is not fully established and perhaps never will be? If the house should no longer exist, how will the lady survive? And, indeed, the house may not exist much longer because there are no Protestants nearby for it to minister to.

Bishop: These reasons are no good. If you do not make her do as I have said, I will degrade and suspend you.

The bishop's manner surprised Father La Combe, yet he knew that suspension did not hinge on such capricious commands.

Father: My lord, I am ready to suffer not only the suspension, but even death, rather than do anything against my conscience.

Father La Combe told me this so I would take proper precautions because he was going off to Rome to be examined by his superiors.

In the meantime, I'd received a letter informing me that the nun at Thonon who cared for my daughter had fallen sick and wanted me to come. I showed this letter to the sisters of the house, telling them I was going. I would return only if they stopped taunting me and left Father La Combe in peace. Instead, they stopped my letters and sent libelous messages against me around the country. So after almost a year with the sisters at Gex, I went to stay at the convent at Thonon.

Moving to Thonon

Life at the convent in Thonon with Marie Jeanne was tranquil. She had forgotten her French and had acquired disagreeable manners among the little girls from the mountains. Yet her wit, good sense, and judgment surprised me, and her disposition was good.

My half sister, who was a nun, got permission to come to stay with me at the convent at Thonon. She helped educate my daughter, but she had frequent disputes with the tutor. Both of these women were gifted instructors, but I could not bring peace to the situation. In this, I saw clearly that the gifts God gives us do not make us good servants unless we use them with deep humility. Dying to ourselves is more beneficial.

As the debates between these two grew more harsh, Marie Jeanne (only six and a half years old) found ways of pleasing them both, doing her exercises twice—first with one, then with the other. This didn't last long, however, because her tutor neglected her. My half sister tried to overcome her moodiness, but it was difficult to bear them both. The situation taught me to love everyone in God, who gives us the ability to bear our neighbors' faults.

O, my God, how true it is that we may have of Thy gifts, and yet be very imperfect and full of ourselves!

Sparring with the Bishop

Just as I arrived at the convent at Thonon, an aged, pious priest told me that he had a vision about me. He had seen a woman in a boat on the lake. The Bishop of Geneva and some priests tried to sink her boat and drown her. The woman seemed to drown but then reappeared, and they kept pursuing her. This woman was always calm. He concluded the bishop would persecute me without interruption.

The aged priest was right. The persecution became more violent, but the Bishop of Geneva was still civil as he prevailed upon me to join the sisters at Gex and donate my money to them. They worried that I would take back my donation to the sisters if I returned to France, but they were mistaken. I did not love my money, but the poverty of Jesus Christ.

The bishop and the priest who had started the persecution also continued to intercept my mail and turn people in France against me. The priest had at this point twenty-two intercepted letters, opened and sitting on his table. One included a power of attorney for me to sign, which they finally did forward to me after putting a new covering on it. The bishop wrote to Father de la Mothe and drew him into this plan, which wasn't difficult because he was already displeased with me. Not only had I not provided a pension for him, but I also did not take his advice in everything.

The only letters I received then came from Father de la Mothe. I answered them as best I could, but this only irritated him more. The bishop treated me outwardly with respect while at the same time he wrote slanderous letters about me to influential friends in Paris. The sisters at Gex did the same. I wasn't well enough to return to France to tell my friends the truth, so our Lord enabled me to suffer everything without defending myself.

I assume this was from Thee, O Lord. Without Thy permission, he was not capable of such inappropriate conduct.

After Easter in 1682 the Bishop of Geneva came to Thonon. When I spoke to him, he seemed to agree with me. I gave him the same reasons against my joining the New Catholics at Gex and then appealed to him, "When you reply this time, think of nothing but God." Confused, he said, "In light of that, I cannot advise you. But do good to this house." I promised him to do that. (Having received my pension, I sent a hundred gold coins to Gex, planning to do so as long as I should be in the diocese.)

The bishop then told me, "Father La Combe is a true servant of God, but when I tell others this, they say I'm mistaken and he will become insane within six months." He also talked of how well the nuns progressed under Father La Combe's care and instruction. So I told him that he ought to listen to God within himself, not to others. The bishop acknowledged this was right, yet after he left he spoke to others and urged me to return to Gex and become the prioress.

After I spoke with the Bishop of Geneva at Thonon, I wrote to him and to Father de la Mothe, but all my efforts were useless. The more I tried to straighten matters out, the more the priest tried to confound them. So I ceased to meddle.

One day I was told that the slandering priest had won over the praying sister at Gex whom I dearly loved. That hurt like the death of a child. I was also advised how I could win her back, but that human way of acting violated my inward sense of rightness. Except the Lord build the house (or the person or a plan), they that build it labor in vain (Ps. 127:1). And God provided, for she did not yield to this deceitful man—she even thwarted his plans. How good God is! She might not have wavered if she'd been with me, but God led her without my interference.

Father de la Mothe wrote me that I was rebelling against my bishop, staying in his diocese only to give him pain. Indeed, I was useless there so long as the bishop was against me. I did what I could to please the bishop, but nothing pleased him except my joining the sisters at Gex, and I knew God was not calling me to that. This, along with the poor education Marie Jeanne was receiving, tore at my heart.

During this time Father La Combe was at Rome, where he was received with honor and his doctrine was highly respected. I hoped that on his return he would bring everything into order, yet I left it all to God.

[Historical records cite Jeanne Guyon's persecutors' motives as varied. Some were jealous of her influence; others did not like the way her teaching on inward prayer highlighted their sin; still others feared her doctrines were too much like Protestantism. These people's opinions affected the bishop so that he became her opponent, perhaps reluctantly.[15]]

Peace in the Storm

In the midst of these violent tempests, my soul was content. People told me hundreds of reckless stories against Father

---

15 Upham, p. 168.

La Combe. The more they said to discredit him, the more respect I felt for him.

Yet life was tranquil for me at Thonon. One of the children would often knock at the door of my apartment, and our Lord would urge me to let myself be interrupted. Through this I saw that God is pleased when we are constantly ready to obey each discovery about His will. This must occur even in the smallest things. My soul seemed then like a leaf or feather which the wind sweeps about.

A soul in a state of calm seeks nothing for itself but all for God. No longer does the soul dabble in impurity through heated emotions or self-seeking, unguarded words. Unless a soul has unity with God, it sullies the work of God. If souls surrendered to God's purification without feeling sorry for themselves, they would make rapid and happy progress! But few are willing to die to self. As soon as the sea is ruffled, they abandon the voyage. Self-love spoils all.

> *The soul that is content in Thee, O God, does not want to know anything but what Thou calls it to. It enjoys divine contentment, more satisfied in a lowly place than on a throne. Oh, if I could express what I think of contentment in Thee! But I can only stammer about it.*

10

Miracles in the Midst of Madness

After Father La Combe returned from Rome, he came to see me. He said that all seemed dark and there was no likelihood that God would make use of me in this country. Meanwhile, I had great pain in my eyes because the same sore from the smallpox returned. My head was frightfully swelled, but great was my inward joy. Then my daughter, Marie Jeanne, fell sick and appeared likely to die. My soul, leaving all to God, continued to rest in a quiet and peaceable habitation. It turned out my daughter had smallpox. A physician from Geneva came but saw no hope. Father La Combe visited and prayed with her, and she soon recovered.

Many other smaller miracles occurred. Once, when I sent to Paris for a bundle of things for Marie Jeanne, I heard they were lost on the lake. The man who had taken charge of them searched a month for them without success. At the end of three months they were brought to me, having been found in the house of a man who had not opened them and who didn't know who brought them there.

Another time, when I sent for my annual salary, the person who was to receive cash for the bill of exchange put the money in two bags on horseback and gave the horse to a little boy to lead, forgetting the money was there. The money fell from the horse in the middle of the market at Geneva. I happened to arrive at that moment at the street in Geneva and sprang from my litter to find my money! What surprised me was that a great crowd was present and hadn't seen it. These many miraculous occurrences showed me the continual protection of God.

> *O God, if we do not let any of the day's moments become removed from Thee, we do not fall. As a dislocated bone gives pain till it is restored to its proper place, so troubles in life come from the soul not abiding with Thee— not being content in Thee and what Thou allows from moment to moment. If people knew this secret, they would all be fully content.*

The Bishop of Geneva did not change his behavior. He would write me to thank me for my donations to the house at Gex, yet tell others I gave nothing to that house. He wrote to the convent in Thonon where I lived and ordered the sisters to stop me from speaking with Father La Combe. The superior of the house, the prioress, and the community were so irritated at this order that they couldn't enforce it. They told the bishop that I saw the Father only at confession and that they were so uplifted by me that they were happy to have me and thought me a great blessing from God.

The bishop was not pleased that the Ursuline sisters at Thonon loved me. He said I was trying to win people over against him and he wanted me to leave his diocese. This troubled

these good Ursuline sisters, but I was content in the will of
God. When abiding in God, all circumstances are equal and
nothing bothers us. To be ruffled over gossip is a pity. It is our
self-love that convinces us we ought to worry.

On Retreat

To find relief from the fatigue of continual conversation, I
asked Father La Combe to allow me a retreat. It was then that
I let myself be consumed by God's love all day long. I also felt
the tug to be a spiritual mother—to help souls. I told this to
Father La Combe, and it touched the innermost places of his
heart. Our Lord showed me He had chosen Father La Combe
to honor Him in a special way. God would lead him through
the death of his old self. He would use me to cause Father La
Combe to travel the road I had that I might help others. With
joy I would see my spiritual children surpass their mother.

In this retreat I felt a strong urge to write, but I had no idea
what to write about. This divine impulse was so full of grace
that I told Father La Combe about it. He replied that he had
sensed a strong impulse to command me to write and asked,
"But what will you write?" I replied, "I don't know and don't
desire to know. I leave it to God to direct me." As I picked up
the pen, I still didn't know what to write. When I began, mate-
rial flowed—copiously, impetuously. I wrote an entire work on
the interior path of faith, comparing it with streams and rivers.

At this time the Lord possessed my soul so strongly that I
passed days without speaking. He became more and more the
absolute master of my heart. This did not hinder me from helping my sister and the others in the house.

Thou, O God, allow us to be possessed by Thee, who hold us so closely to Thyself in an inexpressible manner.

A New Gift Appears

I began to sense that the power to heal rested in me. I experienced what our Lord said when the woman afflicted with the flow of blood touched him: "Someone touched me; I know power has gone out from me" (Luke 8:45, 46). Jesus Christ caused that healing power to flow through me by means of His Word.

Yet God respects the freedom of people. At times I said, "Be healed" or "Be free from your troubles," and such persons acquiesced. The Word was effective, and they were healed. At other times, they resisted (I shall be healed only when it pleases God) or doubted in despair (I cannot be healed. I will not get better). Then the Word had no effect. When the power went out but the person did not say yes to God, I felt it suspended. That gave me pain. Healing is powerful, yet the least doubt in people stops it.

For example, my sister brought me a maid, La Gautiere,[16] whom I believe God wanted me to help but not without inconvenience to myself. The Lord had conferred special gifts on her that made people say she was a saint. In our time together she saw the difference between sanctity which consists of using her gifts and sanctity which comes from death to self, even death to our gifts.

This girl fell terribly sick and remained that way for some time. One day, after dinner, I was moved to say to her, "Rise,

---

16 This maid is named in Upham, pp. 380, 468.

and be well." She got up and was cured. The nuns were astonished to see her walking and decided she hadn't really been sick but only imagined she had.

Also, a good nun who was tormented by violent temptation explained her problem to a seemingly spiritual sister, but this sister rejected her, saying, "Since you're that way, don't come near me." In frightful distress, this girl came to me thinking she was cursed because of the sister's words. I consoled her, and our Lord relieved her torment. I sensed that the sister who rejected her would fall into a state worse than hers.

This "spiritual" sister then came to me, pleased with herself, saying she abhorred people falling into temptation. As for herself, she never had a bad thought. I said to her, "My sister, I wish you understood the pain you caused her." She gave me an arrogant reply, but that night she fell into as violent a temptation as any known. Then she acknowledged her weakness and need for God's grace.

God Speaking in My Sickness

I then fell sick to the edge of my life. Yet in this strange sickness that lasted more than six months, I saw what God planned for me. The world would rage against me with no one defending me, but God would give me vast numbers of children through this cross. He showed me how the devil was going to stir up outrageous persecution against prayer, yet God would also use that persecution to establish prayer. I left it to God to do whatever He pleased and placed myself in His divine will.

I also saw how He would guide me into the wilderness where He would nourish me. The wings for this journey would be the surrender of my whole self to His holy will. At present, I am in that wilderness, separated from the world in my imprisonment. Part of what was shown me is already accomplished. Can I ever express the mercies which my God has given me?

In this sickness, I fell into lengthy, violent convulsions. Since everyone thought I was dying, Father La Combe knelt at my bedside to give me the last rites, when God inspired him to lift up his hands and command death to let go of me. Those in my room—it was almost full—say that death seemed to be stopped instantly. Thus God raised me up again.

Also during this extraordinary sickness, the Lord gradually showed me He has another way for souls to converse—in profound silence. Whenever Father La Combe entered the room, I could speak to him only in silence. Our hearts spoke to each other, communicating grace without words. It was like going to a new country, both for him and for me, but it was so obviously divine I cannot describe it. We passed many hours in this silence, always communicative, without uttering one word. This is one way the heavenly Word reduces souls into unity with itself. I was later able to communicate this way with other souls, but it was one-way communication only. I imparted grace to them, but I received nothing from them. With Father La Combe, there was a back and forth communication of grace.

Throughout this long sickness, I became entirely occupied by the love of God. It seemed as if my heart never came out of that divine ocean, having been drawn into it through crosses and deaths! Jesus was then living in me, and I lived no more.

I saw I would live as Jesus did: "The foxes have holes, and the birds of the air have nests; but the Son of Man hath no where to lay His head" (Matt. 8:20). I have since experienced this—no home or friends, only relatives who renounced me and others who persecuted me. I could say with David: "For thy sake I have borne reproach; shame hath covered my face; I am become a stranger to my brethren, and an alien unto my mother's children; and the reproaches of them, and despised of the people" (Ps. 69:7–9).

It was also at this time that our Lord put it into the heart of Father La Combe to establish a hospital there in Thonon for the poor who were sick, establishing a group of women who could help them. (We had these institutions in France, but there were none so far in Thonon.) A man in town donated rooms, and we dedicated this little establishment to Jesus. God used my pension to purchase the first beds, and others joined us so that it included twelve beds and three helpers who consecrated themselves to serve the poor patients for no pay. I supplied ointments and medicine.

Yet this charity drew upon us new persecutions. The Bishop of Geneva was offended by our charity, saying it made people think favorably of me and my ideas of the interior life with God. He openly declared he could not "bear to have me in his diocese," although I had done nothing but good. He then began harassing the good women who had been my assistants in the charity.

Leaving the Refuge of Thonon

My sickness and pain continued even longer, and some thought the air of the lake (probably Lake Geneva) where the convent was situated was not healthy for me. I had been in Thonon with the Ursuline sisters for about two and a half years, in peace and quiet, but I had to leave. Father La Combe left to be a counselor under the Bishop of Verceil, and I left with Marie Jeanne and La Gautiere, the maid my sister had brought, who was a pleasure to me.

I left Thonon and went to a house farther from the lake. It was a ramshackle place with only one chimney for heat. I gave the largest room to Marie Jeanne and La Gautiere, who took care of her. I lodged in a little hole with straw that required me to use a ladder to get to it. We had no other furniture but our beds, so I brought some straw chairs and earthenware. Never did I enjoy more contentment than in this little hole, which conformed to the state of Jesus Christ. I set us up, hoping to stay there a long time, but the devil did not leave me long in such sweet peace.

Trouble was stirred up against me. People threw stones at my windows. I put in a garden, but people came in the night, tore it up, broke down the arbor, and turned over everything in it. Then they tried to break down the door. In spite of this mistreatment, I thought myself happier there than any queen on earth, but my persecutors insisted I leave the diocese and condemned the good I did. I wondered where I would go.

During my illness, the Marchioness of Prunai, sister of the chief Secretary of State to the Duke of Savoy, sent an express letter inviting me to stay with her. At that time, I was not well enough to come, but I wanted to visit her because I admired this devout lady. She had left the splendor of the royal court for the silent satisfaction of giving herself to God. For twenty-two years she had refused offers of marriage so she could consecrate herself to our Lord entirely. When she knew I'd had to leave Thonon, she invited Father La Combe to visit her at Turin and to bring me with him.

I believed her invitation to be the will of God—that perhaps He was drawing us out of the persecution we labored under. Father La Combe then decided to take me to Turin, and from there he would go on to Verceil. (Both of these cities are located across the Alps Mountains in present-day Italy.)

To keep our enemies from slandering Father La Combe for traveling with me, a single woman, I also took a well-known theology teacher with us. The men rode horses, and I hired a carriage for Marie Jeanne, La Gautiere, and myself. But our critics wrote to friends and authorities in Paris with a hundred ridiculous stories and disgusting jokes about how Father La Combe and I traveled alone from province to province. My half brother, Father de la Mothe, was most active in uttering them, but we did not defend ourselves.

After we arrived at Turin, the Bishop of Geneva wrote letters against us. Then my eldest son came to say my mother-in-law had died and he had sold all our possessions without consulting me. Nor was I asked about the guardian chosen for my younger son. This hurt me deeply.

Yet, Thou, O God, esteemed me useful when others rejected me. In the midst of these persecutions Thou led me to many places to guide souls.

11

Guiding Souls

During my stay at Turin, our Lord helped me understand more about the state of souls. For example, a great servant of God came to Father La Combe to confess and reported wonderful details of her spiritual life. I happened to see her at the confessional, and Father La Combe remarked how he had been edified by her. He even said she had a dedication he had not seen in me. I rejoiced he had met a holy soul.

As I was returning, the Lord showed me how she was only beginning her walk with God, and I mentioned this to him. He said I spoke out of pride, but after that he discovered by her behavior that this woman was very different from what she had said.

Growing in Wisdom

Many times Father La Combe would tell me I was speaking conceited, obstinate opinions, and then he would become angry with me. Then he would change his mind and urge me to continue with God as I had. Sometimes he tried to conceal these negative feelings, but I detected them even from a distance. He and I always knew how the other one felt. He wrote me many times, "When I stand well with God, I find I am well with you. When I am not well with Him, I find I am at odds with you also." We saw how God worked through our unity.

One night in a dream our Lord showed me that God was giving me the gift of discernment of spirits, helping me to see what was truly from Him and reject what was not. Discernment is different from common methods of judging. It doesn't rely on outward information, but on His inward gift alone. Discernment is not natural sympathy or hostility. Indeed, Our Lord had to destroy in me every sort of natural hostility. The soul must be pure, depending on God alone, that all people and events be experienced in Him. As I saw a soul became inwardly purified, my pain decreased until the Lord let me know that person's inward state was changing. Inward pain for souls upset me much more than outward persecutions.

During my stay in Turin with the Marchioness of Prunai, she began viewing me coldly because she considered the child-like simplicity of my spiritual life to be stupidity. She also thought her spirituality more advanced than it was (for she had suffered so few tests). Yet when I prophesied certain events about her household which came true, she became friendly again, believing Christ lived in me. For family reasons, the Marchioness was forced to leave Turin and go to live on her estate. She asked me to go with her, but the education of my daughter did not permit it. To stay at Turin without the Marchioness seemed improper, so I didn't know which way to turn.

The Bishop of Verceil (with whom Father La Combe was) invited me to come, promising me protection. But because of those disgusting jokes made about Father La Combe and me, I would not have it appear that I was going after him. He agreed with me. If we had both believed my going there to be the will of God, however, we would have overlooked that problem. God kept us both in great dependence on His orders.

"Children" at Grenoble

As I was deciding where to go from Turin, Father La Combe came suddenly from Verceil, saying I must return to Paris without delay. "Set off tomorrow morning," he urged me. This news startled me. I didn't want to return to a place where I had been vilified, especially by my family who had gossiped about my journey to Turin in such a disgusting way. But without offering a single word, I set off with Marie Jeanne and La Gautiere, my sweet maid.

At Grenoble (a French city one hundred miles northwest of Turin), I spent a few days with a lady friend, an eminent servant of God. She and Father La Combe urged me to go no further because God would glorify Himself in me in Grenoble. The good father then returned to Verceil, and I saw myself as a child to be led by Providence. Since the inn was full, I stayed at the house of a widow. I placed my daughter in a convent and resolved to spend all my time in solitude surrendering myself to be possessed by God.

I visited no one at Grenoble, yet a few days after my arrival several persons came to see me, explaining their desire to be devoted to God. I saw that God wanted to use me to help others in this way. I discerned the condition of their souls so well that they were surprised and exclaimed I gave them "the very thing they needed." It was God who did these things.

So many souls in Grenoble gave their whole hearts to God. Girls of twelve and thirteen years of age worked industriously all day and enjoyed communion with God at the same time. Not all of the poorer girls could read, so they paired off so that one read prayers to the other while they both worked. A poor laundress who had five children and a husband with a paralyzed arm (disfigured worse in heart than body—he beat her with his good arm) supported her family, displaying the patience and prayer life of an angel. Amid her suffering and poverty, she practiced the presence of God with a tranquil mind. A shop-keeper and a locksmith were also touched by God and took turns reading prayers and Scripture to the laundress.

These people sent others to me until I was occupied from early in the morning until late in the evening, speaking to people of the Lord. People flocked on all sides from far and near—friars, priests, men of the world, maids, wives, widows. I saw the inward state of each one so clearly, and the Lord supplied me with what was appropriate and helpful to them all. They were quickly able to pray—a gift God gave them. The more advanced of these souls found God's unfathomable grace communicated to them in silence. Others found a soothing comfort. God granted great favors to all who came in sincerity.

To those who did not come in sincerity, I was unable to utter even a syllable. If they came to watch my words and criticize me, I could not speak even when I tried. God would not let me. So they said, "People are fools to see that lady. She cannot speak." After they left, someone warned me they were trying to trick me. I told them how the Lord had warned me in advance.

What I spoke seemed to flow from the fountain, and I was only an instrument of God. Yet even in applause, I knew persecutions would come. Today those who say, "Blessed is he who comes in the name of the Lord," will soon cry out, "Away with him, crucify him." When a friend spoke of how people respected me, I said to her, "Watch. You will hear curses come out of the same mouths which now bless me."

It was in Grenoble I sensed a motherhood beyond my previous experiences. Some seemed to be given to me as children. Watching any who slipped cost me inward pain, for they gave up at the point of dying to themselves.

My friend had seen all this mothering of souls in a dream before I came there. She saw the Lord giving me an infinite number of children wearing the same clothing, bearing on their clothes the marks of sincerity and innocence. She thought that meant I was coming to take care of the children of the hospital. But as soon as she told me, I discerned that the dream meant our Lord would give me a great number of spiritual children.

The Book-burning Friars

A certain order of friars in Grenoble had burned all books relating to silence and inward prayer. Once these friars beat a man with sticks in the street because he prayed extemporaneously in the evenings. Those whose lives had become spotless through prayer were driven to the despair.

The book-burning friars sent for the poor laundress and threatened her, saying she had to stop praying. They told her only churchmen could pray and that she was overstepping her bounds. She replied that Christ commanded all to pray and that what He said to His listeners then, He said to all (Mark 13:33, 37). She explained that without prayer she could not support her crosses and poverty, that formerly she had lived without prayer and had been wicked. Since she'd begun praying, she had loved God with all her soul.

Then this laundress proposed an experiment: Take twenty persons who never prayed and twenty who diligently prayed and look at their lives. That, she said, would recommend prayer for all! Her words only irritated them. They told her she had no promise of heaven until she stopped praying. She replied that her salvation depended on Christ. Then they gathered all the books on prayer and burned them in the public square. The town arose in an uproar.

After that a doctor came and laid his heart open to me, saying that he was experienced in the spiritual life but needed more courage and faithfulness. One time he brought me some of his companions, who happened to be friars of the order who were burning books and persecuting people. Yet they too were interested in inward prayer, and the Lord took hold of them all. I was thrilled to see how the Lord used them to make amends for the damages of their brothers.

Among this order of friars, both the superiors and the master of the novices had declared against me because they were mortified that so many should flock to a woman for help. From their viewpoint, God could not house the gift of prayer in so low a vessel as a woman. (From God's viewpoint, He showed great grace in using me.)

Yet the doctor persuaded one of the friar's superiors to see me. In that meeting, our Lord arranged it so that this superior found something in my words that took hold of him. He became convinced of the importance of inward prayer and began dispersing the same books his friars had destroyed.

*Oh, how wonderful art Thou, my God! In all Thy
ways how wise, in all Thy conduct how full of love! How
well Thou can frustrate the false wisdom of men and
triumph over their useless pride!*

Among these friars were many novices. The eldest grew
uneasy under his calling and didn't know what to do. He was so
troubled he couldn't read, study, pray, or work. His companion
brought him to me. We spoke awhile together, and the Lord
showed me his difficulty. I told him and he began practicing
prayer of the heart. As I spoke to him, his soul drank in God's
grace as the parched ground does the gentle rain. He felt
relieved of his inward pain before he left the room.

This novice then began performing his duties and devo-
tions joyfully, which before he had done with reluctance and
disgust. He was so changed that the other novices scarcely knew
him. He was astonished that prayer could give him grace and
peace toward his tasks and toward himself. He gradually
brought me all the novices, all of whom found grace through
prayer, though differently, according to their different tempera-
ments. Never was there a more flourishing novitiate.

The other superior of these book-burning friars and the
master of the novices could not stop exclaiming over the change
in their novices, though they didn't know the cause. One day, as
they were speaking of it to one of the friars, he said, "My
fathers, if you will permit me, I will tell you the reason. It is the
lady you have criticized. You do not know her, but God has used
her for your benefit." Then both the superior and the master of
the novices submitted humbly to practice prayer in a way
explained in a little book the Lord inspired me to write, *A Short*

and Very Easy Method of Prayer (now titled, Experiencing the Depths of Jesus Christ). They reaped such benefit from it that this superior said to me, "I am become quite a new man. I could not practice prayer before because I had grown dull and exhausted. But now I pray easily with a sense of the presence of God." And the master of the novices said, "I have been a friar these forty years and can truly say that I never knew how to pray. I have never known or tasted God as I have since I read that little book."

These friars then re-established prayer, bringing a hundred times more books of prayer than those which their brothers burned. The hand of God appeared to me wonderfully in these things.

More Souls to Be Guided

A sister of a monastery had been in a deep depression for eight years, unrelieved by anyone. Her spiritual director increased it by offering remedies which made it worse. I heard about this but did not go to that monastery because I didn't go places unless I was sent for. I didn't want to intrude, and I wanted the will of God to rule. I was surprised that at eight o' clock at night someone came for me from the prioress. The poor girl had grabbed a knife to kill herself because she was so distraught at not having found a remedy for her depression. When the knife fell out of her hand, her visitor advised her to speak to me.

Our Lord revealed to me her problem and that He wanted her to surrender herself to Him, instead of resisting Him as the remedies offered her had made her do. I helped draw her into this surrender, and she at once entered a peace of paradise. Her pains and troubles were instantly banished and never returned again. She changed so much that she is now the admiration of the community. Our Lord gave her a great gift of prayer and His continual presence.

There at Grenoble, I was especially moved to read the Holy Scriptures. When I began, I felt impelled to write the passage. Instantly I understood it and wrote down an explanation. Light poured in, and I found latent treasures of wisdom and knowledge. Before I wrote, I didn't know what I was going to write. After I'd written, I couldn't remember what I'd written. I used no other book but the Bible. When writing on the Old Testament or New Testament, I referred to passages in the other, but I never had to search for them; I just knew them. The only time I had to write was at night, leaving me only a few hours to sleep.

I continued writing with a great swiftness. My hand could scarcely follow the Spirit's leading fast enough. A diligent transcriber could not copy in five days what I wrote in one night. Whatever is good in it comes from God only. Whatever is otherwise is from myself. In the day I scarcely had time to eat because of the vast numbers of people who came thronging to me.

In the meantime, some priests became uneasy, saying I was taking their jobs and I should not meddle in helping souls. This would have been right if I had been pushing myself forward, but I was not. People came to me; I didn't go to them.

Did thou not, O my God, turn me a hundred ways to test whether I was without fear through every trial or whether I still had some little interest for myself?

12

No Place to Lay My Head

While I was still in Grenoble, a poor girl who worked as a laborer came to me full of sorrow and said, "Alas, I have seen you like a lamb in the midst of a troop of furious wolves. A frightful crowd of people drew swords to destroy you. You didn't look surprised and didn't defend yourself. No one stood up to defend you."

Some days after, lies began to spread about me. The Bishop of Geneva had sent his nephew to go from house to house criticizing me. Some said I was a sorceress, attracting souls by diabolical power. The charity I gave was supposedly false money.

As the tempest increased every day, friends advised me to withdraw from Grenoble. An assistant to the Bishop of Grenoble persuaded me to go to Marseilles to let the storm pass. He thought I would be received well there, and Father La Combe gave his consent. Others invited me—the Bishop of Verceil and the Marchioness of Prunai (now my good friend)—but I followed the instructions of Father La Combe.

O Lord, it seems that Thou made me to bring souls into union with Thee. Thou hast brought wonderful outcomes to my words, forming Jesus Christ in the souls of others. Thou controlled me and made me say what Thou pleased.

Gaining Souls in the Midst of Crosses

My maid, La Gautiere, and a young woman of Grenoble whom I'd helped accompanied me by boat down the Rhone River. We arrived at Marseilles (one of France's Mediterranean seaports) at ten o'clock in the morning. By that afternoon, there was a commotion against me. (This was a quick fulfillment of the poor laborer girl's prophecy.) Some went to the Bishop of Marseilles to say I should be banished from the city because of my book, *A Short and Very Easy Method of Prayer*. Yet the bishop liked the book. He sent for me, receiving me with respect and begging my pardon for the tumult. He asked me to stay in Marseilles and assured me he would protect me. He even asked where I lodged that he might come to see me.

Still, this commotion was not squelched. I received offensive letters from people who had never met me. I saw how the Lord was taking from me every place to dwell, just as Jesus had not a place to lay His head.

During these eight days in Marseilles, I helped support some good souls. One priest followed me to my lodgings after church. He told me the Lord inspired him to talk to me about his inward state. He spoke with such simplicity and humility, and the Lord gave him all he needed through me. He was then filled with joy and thankful words to God.

Where Should I Turn?

From Marseilles, I did not know where or how we should go. I could not return to Grenoble where I had left my daughter in a convent. Father La Combe did not think I should go to Paris. So we took a coach with the plan to see the Marchioness of Prunai in Turin, which was, I thought, the most honorable refuge. I decided to pass through Nice on the seashore on my way to her home, but when we arrived there I was surprised to learn the coach could not pass over the mountains (the Maritime Alps) to Turin.

Again, I didn't know where to go—bewildered, forsaken of everybody, and not knowing what God required of me. My confusion and my crosses seemed to increase. I saw myself without refuge, wandering as a vagabond. I stared at the tradesmen in their shops, who seemed so happy in their own dwellings where they could rest. Nothing seemed harder than this wandering life to me, who naturally loved manners and respectability.

Then someone told me that the next day a sloop would set off by sea to Genoa, but they would let us get off about halfway at Savona (a Mediterranean seaport in what is now Italy). There we could catch a coach to the Marchioness' house in Turin. I had no other choice, so I consented.

I enjoyed being on the sea. I said within myself, "If it be the Lord's pleasure to plunge me in the waves, I shall gladly perish in them." A storm arose that endangered our small boat, and the unrelenting waves tossed us without mercy, reminding me of the slanders I'd suffered. As our boat was beaten and bandied by the waters, my heart was at peace, and I wondered if the mutinous waves would supply me a grave.

I saw a rock jutting up from the sea and thought of living on some uninhabited island. That would end my disgraces and help me be willing to do God's will. Yet God designed a prison far different from a rock and another banishment than that of the uninhabited island.

The storm took us off course so that instead of a short day's voyage, it took eleven days. We could not land at Savona and were forced to go on to Genoa, arriving there in a week before Easter.

The people in Genoa insulted us because we were French and French soldiers had recently bombarded their city. Afterward, the city's chief magistrate had left the city and taken all the coaches with him, so I could not get a coach to Turin where the Marchioness of Prunai lived. I was forced to stay in Genoa several days. The people there demanded outrageous fees and I had little money left, but my confidence in Providence could not be exhausted.

It was three days until Easter, and I begged with great earnestness for a carriage at any price to take us to Turin so we could pass the feast of Easter with the Marchioness. I could scarcely get myself to be understood. They finally brought me a shabby coach with lame mules and told me they would charge me an enormous sum and take us only as far as to Verceil, fifty miles west of Turin. No one would take us to Turin. This upset me greatly, but the place was so full of greed and cheating, I had no choice. Our little company set out for Verceil.

Protected Over and Over

Our mule team driver was a brutal man, treating us coarsely because we were French. At one point, we passed through a woods infested with robbers. The mule team driver was afraid and told us that if we met these robbers, they would murder us. Scarcely had he uttered these words when four armed men appeared, who immediately stopped us. The driver was frightened, but I prayed with a smile on my face for I had no fear. Since I hadn't died at sea, I could die this way.

The robbers moved toward the coach, and as soon as I greeted them, they seemed to change their plans. They returned my greeting respectfully and spoke with a compassion unusual to those who steal from you. Then they left. I was immediately struck to the heart with conviction that this was a stroke of God's hand, who had different plans for me than to die by the hands of robbers.

As evening drew near, the mule team driver began bullying me, seeing I was accompanied by no men. Instead of taking us to the inn as was customary, he took us to a mill with one room in which we were to stay with the millers and mule team drivers. They tried to force us to stay there, but I objected. When he refused to take us to the inn, we walked at ten o'clock at night carrying our luggage, going almost a mile in the dark, not knowing the way, crossing a portion of the woods infested with robbers.

The driver, seeing us set off on foot, hooted after us saying abusive things. I bore this embarrassment, but not without feeling it. As we walked, I resigned myself to the will of God, and it became easier. We were well received at the inn, and the good people there accommodated us. The next morning we returned on foot to the carriage where the driver showered us with fresh insults.

When the coach arrived at Alexandria (near Milan), the landlady did not want us to stop. She'd heard the passengers were women and assumed we were a certain sort of women. She protested, but the driver was determined to set us down. Their dispute grew so hot that a mob gathered and the officers of the garrison came. I asked the driver to take us elsewhere, but he insisted it was her job to take us in. Finally, he brought her to the coach. As soon as she had looked at us, she relented as the robbers had done.

No sooner had we gotten out of the coach than she said, "Shut yourselves in the room and do not move an inch so my son will not know you are here. If he hears you, he will kill you." She said it with so such force that I should have died on the spot with fear. The two poor girls with me were terrified. When anyone came near the place, they thought the son was coming to kill us. We lay there, between life and death, until the next day when we learned the story. A few days before, an unseemly woman murdered a man of great respect. This had cost the woman's son a heavy fine and ruined him. He had sworn to kill any woman who lodged at the house in the future.

The Bishop of Verceil, My Friend

After these misadventures, we arrived at Verceil. Father La Combe met us in a strange fret. He said everyone would think I came chasing after him and that would injure his good reputation. His coolness doubled my pain. I asked him if he required me to leave, because if he did I would go. He said he didn't know if the Bishop of Verceil would welcome my arrival since he'd expected me for so long but I had not come.

It seemed to me then as if I had been rejected from the face of the earth, unable to find refuge, as if all creatures joined together to crush me. I could not sleep that night at the inn, not knowing what I should do—being persecuted by my enemies and bringing disgrace to my friends.

When the bishop learned of my arrival, his niece brought us to her house, and he came to see me. Though he understood French as poorly as I understood Italian, he and I established a strong friendship, and he said I was like a sister to him. He would often come to pass half an hour with me in speaking of God. He wrote to the Bishop of Marseilles to thank him for protecting me in the persecutions there. He wrote to the Bishop of Grenoble of his regard for me.

The Bishop of Verceil then decided he wanted me to stay there and would not hear of my going to Turin to see the Marchioness. Instead, he invited her to settle in Verceil. He sent Father La Combe to her to urge her to come, and she came readily with her daughter. The bishop hoped to establish a group of devoted souls, but apparently it was not the will of God to establish me there. Rather, it seemed His will to crucify me more.

The fatigue of traveling made the girl I'd brought from Grenoble and me ill. Her relatives were worried that I had persuaded her to make a will in my favor before she died. They were mistaken. Far from desiring the property of others, I had given up my own. Her brother came quickly, asking her to make a will even though she recovered. He wanted her to return with him, but she refused. I advised her to do what her brother desired. In the meantime, he'd made friends with officers of the garrison, telling them that I was treating his sister poorly. They then began saying I was chasing after Father La Combe, and they persecuted him on my account.

This commotion troubled the bishop, but he could not remedy it. Still, our friendship increased everyday because he loved those who loved God. In my sickness, he visited me often, making me little presents. Then his relatives became jealous, saying I was ruining him and would carry his money off to France. The bishop bore these insults, hoping to keep me in his diocese when I recovered.

In Verceil, everything was mixed with crosses, but souls were gained to God. Though I could not understand the language of certain friars nor they understand mine, the Lord helped us comprehend what the other was saying. A Jesuit priest decided to test me once when Father La Combe was out of town. A well educated theologian, he asked me questions and the Lord inspired me to answer him in a manner that surprised and satisfied him. He could not stop speaking of how well I answered.

My sickness grew worse. The bishop was upset by this, but after the doctors told him the bad air there was causing my continual cough and fever, he said he would regretfully allow me to leave. He gave up his plan to establish a group of devoted souls and said, "You were willing to work in the diocese of Geneva, and they persecuted you. I, who would gladly have you, cannot keep you." He wrote to Father de la Mothe, my half brother, that I would come in the spring as soon as the weather would permit.

Toward Paris

At this point, Father de la Mothe asked to have Father La Combe appointed as his assistant. Father La Combe, who did not comprehend the poison under Father de la Mothe's request, consented. The superior ordered Father La Combe to return to Paris, bringing me with him (so the traveling expenses would be covered by me instead of their order). Father La Combe left before me to transact business, waiting for me at the mountain pass where I would most need an escort. The Bishop of Verceil and I parted with sorrow. At his own expense, he sent attendants with me as far as Turin.

I could not pass through Turin without seeing my good friend, the Marchioness of Prunai. She was overjoyed to see me. We made ointments together, and I gave her the secret of my remedies. I encouraged her to establish a hospital in that place, and she did that while we were there.

As soon as Father La Combe was ordered to accompany me to Paris, Father de la Mothe reported to my friends of my supposed attachment for Father La Combe, pretending to pity me for my erring ways. This made people say I ought to put myself under the direction of Father de la Mothe. In the meantime, he disguised the evil of his heart, writing respectful letters to Father La Combe and tender ones to me. He said he "desired to bring his dear sister to Paris, and to serve her in her sickness."

When I was told to come to Paris, the Lord made known to me that my greatest crosses were coming. Father La Combe had a similar sense. He encouraged me to resign myself to God's divine will, even if it meant becoming a victim offered freely. I set off with a spirit of sacrifice to offer myself up to new persecutions, if that pleased my dear Lord. All along the road something within me repeated the words of Paul, "And now, compelled by the Spirit, I am going to Jerusalem, not knowing what will happen to me there. I only know that in every city the Holy Spirit warns me that prison and hardships are facing me. However, I consider my life worth nothing to me, if only I may finish the race and complete the task the Lord Jesus has given me" (Acts 20:22–24, NIV).

When I told this to my most intimate friends, they tried to stop me. They offered to give me money to settle in Verceil, but I could not take it.

O God, it was my duty to sacrifice myself for Thee, who first sacrificed all for me.

13

Peace in the Face of Revenge

I tell the rest of this story only to obey the command given me to omit nothing. I am forced to speak often of my half brother, Father de la Mothe, and wish with all my heart I could suppress what I have to say of him. Though Father de la Mothe may be slandered by what I say, I protest in the presence of God that I am omitting many of his bad actions. If what he did affected only me, I would bury it all. But I tell the truth to vindicate Father La Combe, cruelly oppressed and grievously crushed by slanders and long imprisonments.

I fetched Marie Jeanne, my daughter, in Grenoble and arrived at Paris on St. Magdalene's Eve, 1686, exactly five years after my departure from that city. I'd left to win souls at Geneva, but instead I guided both wandering and pious souls in several cities.

Scarcely had I arrived, when I discovered the dark designs entertained against Father La Combe and me. Father de la Mothe conducted the whole tragedy, flattering me to my face while aiming sharp wounds at my back. He and his associates wanted me to go to my native town, Montargis (about sixty-five miles south of Paris). But if I fled to my hometown, it would appear I was admitting guilt to the charges they were going to present, helping them get guardianship of my children and control of the rest of my fortune and estate. I decided I would not appeal to the law. If they were determined to take from me what little I had not given up, I would surrender it to them. I was willing to be poor in imitation of our Lord Jesus Christ.

In eternity Thou wilt show who are Thy true friends.
Nothing pleases Thee but those who conform to Jesus Christ
and bear His character.

Revenge Against My Friend

Father de la Mothe and my family tormented Father La Combe out of rage and revenge, because he, as my spiritual director, did not force me to do what they wanted. I believe my half brother was also jealous of La Combe's magnificent preaching.

For example, I'd given Father La Combe a little sum of money (with the consent of his superior) to pay for the entrance of a nun in the convent. I felt obliged to do this because she had, through my influence, left the New Catholics. (This is the young woman who the priest at Gex wanted to win over, but did not.) Father de la Mothe wanted that money and told Father La Combe to force me to give it to him to rebuild a wall for his convent. If he did not, Father de la Mothe said he would make Father La Combe suffer for it. But La Combe, who is always upright, answered that he in good conscience couldn't advise me to do other than what my conscience told me. This further set Father de la Mothe in a mood of revenge.

A man was hired to write defamatory letters, declaring that Father La Combe followed the beliefs of a current group of heretics led by Michael de Molinos. Father de la Mothe carried these accusations to the judge of the ecclesiastical court, who joined in the dark design. They showed them to the archbishop, saying that out of their zeal for God, they were forced to expose this heretic from among their brothers. They included me as a heretic as well.

Then they came up with another fraud to enhance their scheme. They remembered I had been at Marseilles, and so they counterfeited a letter from the Bishop of Marseilles addressed to the Archbishop of Paris. Father de la Mothe showed it to me and said, "Look at this shocking account against you. You have created a scandal with Father La Combe. We have witnesses to prove it."

I replied, "Your story is clever, but you didn't check to see if Father La Combe was also at Marseilles. I do not believe he was ever there in his life. While I was there, Father La Combe was laboring at Verceil."

Father de la Mothe was confused and then questioned Father La Combe, who said he had never been at Marseilles. They were struck with disappointment. They then changed their story to say the letter came not from Marseilles but Seisel. But I had never been to Seisel, so that foiled the scheme.

Every imaginable device was used to terrify me: threats, forged letters, accusations of teaching erroneous doctrines. Since these things failed, Father de la Mothe went public with his accusations against me, standing up in church and saying, "You, my sister, must flee. You are charged with crimes of a deep dye."

I was not moved, but replied with my usual tranquility, "I have publicly dedicated myself to God. If I have offended God, I must be punished to set an example to the world. But if I am innocent, I must not flee." My resolution of purpose surprised him, and then angered him.

Father La Combe was grossly misrepresented to the king and arrested. Although he appeared innocent at his trial and no grounds were found to condemn him, our accusers persuaded the king to believe he was a dangerous man in religious circles. He was then imprisoned for life in a fortress at the Bastille. When his enemies heard the fortress captain respected him and treated him kindly, they had him moved to much worse places.

Thou O God, who beholds everything will reward every man according to his works.

More Counterfeits and Forges

With Father La Combe out of the way, Father de la Mothe tried more than ever to force me to flee. He assured me that if I went to Montargis, my troubles would end. If I did not, however, I should pay for not following his orders. He slandered me wherever he went and had his brothers send me abusive letters, telling me that if I did not take him as my spiritual director, I was undone. (I have these letters still.) Some advised me to pretend to put myself under his guidance and to deceive him, but I could not do this in good conscience.

I endured all this with tranquility. I did not justify or defend myself, but left it entirely to God to do as He pleased. In this, He increased the peace of my soul. At church I heard people criticize me. Some priests even said I should be cast out of the church. I left myself to God, being ready to endure rigorous pains and tortures if such were His will.

Although people were raising their voices against me, God did not fail to make use of me to gain many souls to Himself. The more persecution raged against me, the more children were given to me. The Lord conferred great favors through me, His handmaid.

They then made the king believe I was a heretic, telling him that *A Short and Very Easy Method of Prayer* was a dangerous book. They also said I'd corresponded with the heretic, Michael de Molinos, when in fact, I'd never heard of him until I read about him in the *Gazette*. To support this slander, my handwriting was counterfeited, and a letter was forged in which I supposedly stated I held meetings at my house but had stopped because of Father La Combe's imprisonment. I would presumably hold meetings at other persons' homes if I could avoid being watched. They showed this forged letter to the king, and based on it an order was given for my imprisonment.

In the meantime, Father de la Mothe then came to me when I was extremely ill, pretending to be tender and saying that Father La Combe's case was going well. He wanted the good father to be released from prison, he said, but he needed the certificate I had from the Inquisition, clearing Father La Combe. He promised to deliver it to the authorities.

At first I acted as if it was too difficult to get it. "What!" he said, "Will you be the cause of ruining poor Father La Combe? You have that power in your hands." I yielded, telling my servants to give it to him. A court official later asked me for this certificate to help Father La Combe, and I referred him to Father de la Mothe, but he denied that I'd given it to him. He said of me, "Her brain is disordered, and she imagines things." The messenger returned to me, and the persons tending me in my chamber testified that I'd given it to him. Yet the court could not get it from him.

They waited only for my recovery to cast me into prison. Father de la Mothe told the clerical brothers I had treated him ill. They wrote to me that I was suffering for my crimes and that I should put myself under the control of Father de la Mothe. It was reported I was mad and should be tied up, that I was a monster of pride in not allowing myself to be guided by Father de la Mothe. Such was my daily feast in my extreme pain. Deserted by my friends and oppressed by my enemies, I kept silent, leaving myself to the Lord.

I was then accused of all kinds of scandal, error, sorcery, and sacrilege. As soon as I was well enough to be carried to the church in a chair, I was told I must speak to officials. I spoke with simplicity, and they said they believed what I said. Yet two days later it was reported I had accused many persons, and they used these supposed accusations to banish various persons with whom they were displeased—men of honor whom I had never seen or heard of. One was banished because he said my little book, *A Short and Very Easy Method of Prayer*, was good.

It is remarkable that the book was not condemned, but even reprinted since I have been in prison. Advertisements of it have been posted at the archbishop's palace and all over Paris.

The same day those gentlemen were banished I received a sealed order to go to a convent in the Paris suburb of St. Antoine. The deliverer of the order often witnessed the sorrow of those being banished and was surprised I was so calm. He was so touched he shed tears. And although he was ordered to bring me immediately, he trusted me and gave me the day to myself. Many of my friends came to see me. I could not stand up because I was so weak, having had the fever every night for many weeks before.

Locked Up in a Convent

On January 29, 1688, I went to the Convent of the Visitation of St. Mary's. I hoped the nuns would let Marie Jeanne and La Gautiere stay with me, but I was locked up alone in a chamber. They would not even allow anyone to bring me news of my daughter.

The sisters of the convent were told such frightful things about me that they looked at me with horror. For my jailer, they chose a nun whom they predicted would treat my harshly. She did. They asked me who my priest was (now that Father La Combe was in prison), and so I gave his name, but he denied it. I offered to produce witnesses who saw me at his confessional, but they said they'd caught me in a lie, and I could not be trusted.

My keeper was convinced I was an insane heretic and hypocrite. God alone knows what she made me suffer. As she tried to trap me in my words, I tried to be more exact but that only made it worse. I made more errors and gave her advantages over me. I then stopped trying, thinking this woman would bring me to the scaffold by the false reports she carried to the prioress. I resigned myself to my lot and went back to my tranquil state before God.

Interrogations Begin

High church officials came four times to question me. Our Lord did me the favor of helping me answer much better than if

I had studied. They said that if I had explained myself as well as I had in my book, *A Short and Very Easy Method of Prayer*, I would not have been in trouble. My last examination was about a counterfeit letter, which they read and let me see. I told them the writing was not mine, but they said it was just a copy. The original was elsewhere, they said, but they wouldn't let me see it. When I told them I didn't write the letter nor did I know the person to whom it was addressed, that didn't matter to them. I showed them its inconsistencies, but they wouldn't listen. I was left in the convent two months and treated worse than before. Till then I had hoped that they would see my innocence and do justice by me. But by then I saw that they did not want to find me innocent, but to make me appear guilty.

The official came alone the next time and told me I must not speak of the letter because it was nothing. "It is *not* nothing," I said, "to counterfeit a person's writing and make one appear an enemy of the state!" He replied that they would try to figure out who wrote it, so I gave them the name of the hired forger. The official changed the subject, demanding the papers which I had written on the Scriptures. I told him I would give them up only when I was released from prison.

Although these examinations were confusing, I felt inexpressible satisfaction and joy in suffering and being a prisoner. The confinement of my body made me relish better the freedom of my mind. At times, I felt more in touch with heaven than earth. At that point they took more privileges away from me. I was forced to surrender myself anew and drink the dregs of the bitter draught.

14

In the Hands of God

A few days after the last examination, the official came and gave me freedom to come and go within the convent. My enemies then urged me to consent for my daughter to marry an old friend of the king, a man notorious for his unchristian morals. If I allowed this to happen to my twelve-year-old Marie Jeanne, they promised to release me from prison and to drop all charges. But if I refused, I'd be imprisoned for life or die on the scaffold. In spite of their threats, I could not buy my liberty by sacrificing my daughter.

Soon after my refusal, the officials told the prioress at St. Mary's I must be locked up. She explained that my small chamber was so stuffy and hot—it was July—that without ventilation and shelter from the sun, I would die. They paid no attention. When she asked why I must be so closely confined, they said I'd scandalized the nuns of her house. She protested, saying I'd helped the nuns, and they admired my patience. But nothing changed their minds. The poor woman could not stop crying from hearing words so far from the truth.

Then they sent for me, saying I'd done wretched things in the last month. I asked, "What things?" They would not tell me. I declared God as my witness that I was imprisoned based on forgeries. They faulted me for calling on God, but I said that nothing in the world could hinder me from relying on God's support. I was then confined more closely than at first, until I was at the point of death with a violent fever, stifled with the closeness of the place, and having no one to help me.

Eight months later, I was told I would be released, but the Lord gave me a sense that they were only laying new snares for me. On August 22, 1688 (my birthday), being forty years of age, I awakened with the impression of Jesus Christ agonizing, seeing the council of the Jews against Him. I knew that none but God could deliver me out of prison, and I was satisfied that He would do it one day by His hand. Though I was ignorant of how He would do it, I would leave it wholly to Him.

According to Divine Providence, my case was laid before Madame de Maintenon, who became deeply interested in my story. (She was the king's morganatic wife[17] and exercised great influence over him.) This procured my release, and she became my protector.

Life Under My Protector

Coming out of the convent, I went to the house where my daughter lived. There I lay in bed with a fever for three months

---

[17] Will and Ariel Durant. *The Story of Civilization Vol. VIII* (New York: Simon & Shuster, 1963), p. 685. A morganatic marriage is a valid marriage contracted by a European royal with a person of inferior rank. It is understood that neither she nor any of her children would inherit title or wealth. Upham says their marriage was secret, which might explain why she has also been referred to as the king's mistress. Actually, she refused to be his mistress, which is why the morganatic marriage was necessary.

and had a sore in my eye. Marie Jeanne lived there with her husband, Monsieur Nicholas Fouquet, Count de Vaux. Because she was so young, I stayed with her for two and a half years to help her. Even there my enemies forged documents against me and accused me of holding clandestine meetings. I wanted to steal away to a convent in my hometown, Montargis, but it was discovered and both friends and enemies prevented it.

The family of my daughter's husband were friends of Abbe Francois Fenelon, so I had the opportunity to see him often at her house. We had some conversations on the spiritual life, in which he objected to my experiences, primarily because the heresy of Michael de Molinos also favored simplicity. As heretics made news, simple teaching was distrusted, but I explained everything to him so clearly that he drank fully of my beliefs. This laid the foundation for the persecution he went on to suffer.

After this time, I took a private little house to be alone. Sometimes I had the pleasure of seeing my family and a few particular friends there. Madame de Maintenon, my protector, introduced me to the young ladies of St. Cyr (a charitable institution to educate impoverished young women, founded by Madame de Maintenon[18]), and they told her how they found a great attraction to God in their conversations with me. She was glad, and she saw changes in several who had previously displeased her. She then treated me with much respect, and for three years after she placed great confidence in me.

---

[18] Thomas C. Upham. *Life of Madame Guyon* (London: Allenson & Co., LTD, 1905), p. 332.

But the confidence some of these young ladies placed in me made my persecutors uneasy. They said the ladies paid more attention to me than to them, so I saw the young ladies no more. Instead, I answered the ones who wrote to me, giving my unsealed letters to Madame Maintenon, my protector, to inspect and verify.

I was puzzled by people's responses to Madame de Maintenon's friends (the Countess of G. and the Duchess of M.), who moved from worldly pursuits to godly devotion. How is it that when these ladies pursued entertainments of the world and damaged their families with gambling and buying expensive clothes, nobody said anything against their behavior, but when they left that vain life, I was blamed as if I had ruined them?

In this otherwise tranquil time, I fell sick again, and the doctors ordered me to go to the waters of Bourbon. They determined that I'd been poisoned by my servant and would have died within a few hours without proper help. The servant ran away immediately, and I have never seen him since. (I suffered the effects of the poison for more than seven years.)

Still God kept me ready to sacrifice. I was glad to receive from God's hand whatever might befall me. To try to vindicate myself would have been as useless as punching the air or an imaginary person. When the Lord wills that someone should suffer, He permits even the most virtuous people to be blinded and thereby join in persecuting that person. How often have I said that I fear more the reproach of my conscience than of the condemnation of all men!

Since, O my Lord, I long to conform to Thee, to please
Thee, I am willingly disgraced. I would rather see myself

condemned by everybody than to be honored at the summit
of the world—if it be Your will.

The Examinations of Boussuet, The Bishop of Meaux

At this time I had my first acquaintance with the Bishop of Meaux. I gave him what I had written of this, my story, and he confessed he found in it a rare anointing of God. He spent three days reading it with a constant impression of the presence of God on his mind. I proposed that the bishop examine all my writings, which he took four or five months to do. He then offered his objections, to which I gave answers. From his lack of experience in the inward life, I could not clear up all the difficulties which he found in them. He admitted that church history showed that God sometimes made use of laymen and women to instruct, edify, and help souls.

As the outcry against me became more violent, I requested the appointment of proper persons to examine my life and doctrines, offering to be imprisoned until cleared. My proposal was rejected.

Three commissioners asked me for evidence, so I sent them my two little printed books and commentaries on the Holy Scriptures. By their order, I also wrote a summary of my work to spare them the time and trouble of reading it all. In it, I quoted many approved writers, which showed the conformity of my writings with the church. For some reason, the Bishop of Meaux would never allow my work to be read.

After the examiners found nothing against me, I was still not left in peace. Finally, I offered to spend time in any religious community within the Bishop of Meaux's diocese that he might become better acquainted with me. He agreed, so we left in the depth of winter and were stopped four hours as the coach entered the snow and was almost buried by it in a deep hollow. My maid, La Gautiere, and I got out the coach door and sat on the snow, certain to die if we passed the night there. This poor girl and I were tranquil in our minds, though chilled and soaked with snow, which melted around us. Occasions like these show whether we are perfectly resigned to God or not. After a while, some wagons came up and they pulled us through the snow.

When the bishop heard about our journey, he was astonished that that I had risked my life to obey him so punctually. Yet afterward he denounced our trip as scheming and hypocritical.

So for six months I lived at the convent of St. Mary in Meaux (twenty-five miles northeast of Paris). Six weeks after my arrival, I took a fever. I had not recovered when the bishop visited me and tried to compel me to say I did not believe that Christ had come in the flesh. I answered that I would suffer death before I would sign such a falsehood. Several of the nuns who overheard this conversation defended me with testimonials of my good conduct and sound faith.

Some days later the bishop asked me to sign a statement that I'd fallen into errors, threatening me with persecutions (which I would suffer anyway in the future). I refused to put my name to falsehoods. After I had remained six months at Meaux, he gave me the certificate of approval. He later asked that I return it, but I refused. This enraged him.

Many places of retreat were offered me, but I did not feel free to accept them. I did not want to embarrass anybody or have my escape blamed on friends or family. I decided to stay in

Paris, in a private place with my maid, who was trustworthy and sure, and to hide myself from the world. I did this for five or six months. I passed the day alone reading, working, and praying to God.

During this time, the king decided I should not be put in prison but stay in a convent. But then he was deceived by slanderers who painted me in dark colors. They demanded I go to the prison in the castle in Vincennes, which serves as a military fortress and a prison as well.[19] The king finally consented, so on December 27, 1695, I was arrested and taken to Vincennes.

Life in Prison

I shall not say much of that long persecution, which has created so much talk. Perhaps some will be surprised at my refusing to give the details of the greatest and strongest crosses of my life, after telling about crosses which were less. I thought it proper to tell about the crosses of my youth to show how God proved and tested me.

At Vincennes, I passed my time in great peace, content to live the rest of my life there if that were the will of God. I sang songs of joy, which La Gautiere, who served me, learned by heart as fast as I made them up. Together we sang God's praises. (This faithful maid was arrested and imprisoned with her.[20]) The stones of my prison looked like rubies to me. I loved them more than all the gaudy brilliant stones of the world.

For ten years I experienced a series of imprisonments, and a banishment almost as long, that is still in force today. I have

---

[19] Upham, p. 379.
[20] Upham, p. 380.

borne many crosses and slanders. I have suffered long bouts of painful sicknesses without relief. I have also felt such inward desolation for several months that all I could say was, "My God, my God, why has Thou forsaken me!"

Yet I had no desire that my imprisonment should end before the right time. I loved my chains. I had unspeakable joy and freedom in my rigorous captivity. I was and am tranquil in the midst of a furious tempest which assaults me on every side. The gospel promises to those that leave all for the love of the Lord a "hundred fold now in this time...with persecutions" (Mark 10:30). I have had more than a hundred fold from the Lord as He has taken entire possession of me.

> *My heart was full of the joy which Thou gives to them who love Thee, in the midst of their greatest crosses.*

In the Bastille,[21] when things were carried to the greatest extremes, I said, "O, my God, if Thou art pleased to make me an example to men and angels, Thy holy will be done!" Even in my present banishment, any circumstance appears equal to me, as I have no will of my own. My perseverance comes not from me, but from Him who is my life, so that I can say with the apostle, "It is no more I that live, but Jesus Christ that liveth in me" (Gal. 2:20). It is He in whom I live, move, and have my being.

I never had any resentment against my persecutors, though I knew them well. I love my persecutors with all my heart and pray for them, leaving to God the task of delivering me out of their hands. I make no moves of my own. Jesus Christ said His persecutors had no power except what was given them from

---

21 The infamous prison-fortress destroyed during the French Revolution.

above (John 19:11). One cannot hate the hand God uses to strike us with.

If my chains and my imprisonment upset you, I pray they may urge you to seek nothing but God and to be possessed by God—not by being someone important but by death of your whole self.

Epilogue

When Jeanne Guyon was arrested in 1695, she had lost the help of her protectress, Madame de Maintenon, so influential to King Louis XIV. She was moved from Vincennes, and from 1698 to 1702 she lived in solitary confinement in the notorious Bastille (at the same time and place as the legendary prisoner #64389000, the man in the iron mask). There she endured the most rigorous persecution.

In all, she stayed in prison eight years and was released on the condition that she live in "exile," meaning she was confined to Paris. So at fifty-four, she visited her daughter, Marie Jeanne, but her fame and afflictions forced the courts to change her exile to Blois, a city one hundred miles southwest of Paris. She left off this narrative in December, 1709, though she lived a quiet life for seven more years. She died June 9, 1717, at Blois, in her seventieth year.

In the same year Jeanne Guyon was arrested, the man she poured so much of herself into was appointed archbishop of Cambrai. Abbe Francois Fenelon had been a favorite among the royal court for tutoring and reforming the king's grandson. When he met Jeanne Guyon at her daughter's house, Fenelon was deeply influenced for life.

As the new Archbishop of Cambrai, Fenelon began to vindicate his spiritual mentor by opposing her accuser, Bossuet, the Bishop of Meaux. The bishop was regarded as one of France's finest orators, and had earlier taken Fenelon under his wing on a preaching mission. While Bossuet did a great deal of good, he also was a product of the school of thought that questioned all beliefs and insisted that reason triumph over all—especially Jeanne Guyon's beliefs, which came to be called "quietism."

The controversy between these two men continued for several years, with Bossuet condemning Fenelon's book and the two appearing before Pope Innocent XII. With reluctance, the Pope condemned parts of the book, commenting "that Fenelon erred by loving God too much, Bossuet (the Bishop of Meaux) by loving man too little."[22]

After Fenelon's next book, the Pope tried to elevate Fenelon to cardinal but the king banished him to his diocese, where he earned the reputation of being a good pastor to the people. His defense of Jeanne Guyon cost him the upwardly mobile career he worked so hard for, but no trace of bitterness is found in his writing. He seemed to have grasped well what he learned from God through his friend—to pray from the heart and abandon one's self to God.

22 Jean H. Faurot. "Christian Perfection " (Francois Fenelon) *Christian Spirituality* Magill, Frank N. & McGreal, Ian P., ed. (San Francisco, CA: Harper & Row, 1988), pp. 346.

SEEDSOWERS
800-228-2665   (fax) 866-252-5504
www.seedsowers.com

REVOLUTIONARY BOOKS ON CHURCH LIFE

Beyond Radical *(Edwards)* 8.95
How to Meet In Homes *(Edwards)* 10.95
The Christian Woman...Set Free*(Edwards)* 12.95
When the Church Was Led Only by Laymen *(Edwards)* 5.00
Revolution, The Story of the Early Church *(Edwards)* 12.95
The Silas Diary *(Edwards)* 10.95
The Titus Diary *(Edwards)* 10.95
The Timothy Diary *(Edwards)* 10.95
The Priscilla Diary *(Edwards)* 10.95
The Gaius Diary *(Edwards)* 10.95
Overlooked Christianity *(Edwards)* 12.95
Paul's Way or the Seminary's Way *(Edwards)* .... coming soon
The Shocking Story of the History of Bible Study *(Edwards)* .... coming soon
Why You Should Consider Leaving the Pastorate *(Edwards)* 5.00
The Organic Church vs. The New Testament Church *(Edwards)* 7.50
Problems and Solutions in a House Church *(Edwards)* 7.50
How to Start a House Church From Scratch *(Edwards)* 5.00
Why So Many House Churches Fail and What to Do About It *(Edwards)* 5.00

AN INTRODUCTION TO THE DEEPER CHRISTIAN LIFE

Living by the Highest Life *(Edwards)* 10.95
The Secret to the Christian Life *(Edwards)* 10.95
The Inward Journey *(Edwards)* 12.95

CLASSICS ON THE DEEPER CHRISTIAN LIFE

Experiencing the Depths of Jesus Christ *(Guyon)* 9.95
Practicing His Presence *(Lawrence/Laubach)* 9.95
The Spiritual Guide *(Molinos)* 9.95
Union With God *(Guyon)* 9.95
The Seeking Heart *(Fenelon)* 10.95
Intimacy with Christ *(Guyon)* 10.95
Spiritual Torrents *(Guyon)* 10.95
The Ultimate Intention *(Fromke)* 10.00
One Hundred Days in the Secret Place *(Edwards)* 13.99

IN A CLASS BY ITSELF

The Divine Romance *(Edwards)* 12.99

NEW TESTAMENT

The Story of My Life as Told by Jesus Christ *(Four gospels blended)* 14.95
The Day I was Crucified as Told by Jesus the Christ 14.99
Acts in First Person *(Book of Acts)* 9.95

COMMENTARIES BY JEANNE GUYON

Genesis Commentary 10.95
Exodus Commentary 10.95
Leviticus - Numbers - Deuteronomy Commentaries 12.95
Judges Commentary 7.95
Job Commentary 10.95
Song of Songs *(Song of Solomon Commentary)* 9.95

(2008 prices...subject to change later)

COMMENTARIES BY JEANNE GUYON CONTINUED

Jeremiah Commentary 7.95
James - I John - Revelation Commentaries 12.95

THE CHRONICLES OF HEAVEN *(Edwards)*

Christ Before Creation 8.99
The Beginning 8.99
The Escape 8.99
The Birth 8.99
The Triumph 8.99
The Return 8.99

THE COLLECTED WORKS OF T. AUSTIN-SPARKS

The Centrality of Jesus Christ 19.95
The House of God 29.95
Ministry 29.95
Service 19.95
Spiritual Foundations 29.95
The Things of the Spirit 10.95
Prayer 14.95
The On-High Calling 10.95
Rivers of Living Water 8.95
The Power of His Resurrection 8.95

COMFORT AND HEALING

A Tale of Three Kings *(Edwards)* 8.99
The Prisoner in the Third Cell *(Edwards)* 9.99
Letters to a Devastated Christian *(Edwards)* 8.95
Exquisite Agony *(Edwards)* 9.95
Dear Lillian *(Edwards) paperback* 5.95
Dear Lillian *(Edwards) hardcover* 9.99

OTHER BOOKS ON CHURCH LIFE

Climb the Highest Mountain *(Edwards)* 12.95
The Torch of the Testimony *(Kennedy)* 14.95
The Passing of the Torch *(Chen)* 9.95
Going to Church in the First Century *(Banks)* 6.95
When the Church was Young *(Loosley)* 8.95
Church Unity *(Litzman,Nee,Edwards)* 10.95
Let's Return to Christian Unity *(Kurosaki)* 10.95

CHRISTIAN LIVING

The Christian Woman . . . Set Free *(Edwards)* 12.95
Your Lord Is a Blue Collar Worker *(Edwards)* 7.95
The Autobiography of Jeanne Guyon 19.95
Final Steps in Christian Maturity *(Guyon)* 12.95
Turkeys and Eagles *(Lord)* 9.95
The Life of Jeanne Guyon *(T.C. Upham)* 17.95
Abridged Edition of Guyon's Autobiography *(Johnson)* 10.95
All and Only *(Kilpatrick)* 8.95
Adoration *(Kilpatrick)* 9.95
Bone of His Bone *(Huegel) modernized* 9.95
You Can Witness with Confidence *(Rinker)* 10.95